The Relationship Restoring OCPD Fundamentals

Laying the Foundation
for **Your**
<u>*Successful*</u> ♥ Couples' Interaction
And Recovery

By *Mack W. Ethridge*
OCPD Specialist, NFHR, Inc.

<u>VITALLY</u> IMPORTANT NOTE!

This book is designed to serve as a **Primer** to the author's <u>*numerous*</u> books on Obsessive Compulsive Personality Disorder (OCPD). Particularly, 'OCPD's Only Hope' and 'Escaping Another's OCPD Tyranny'.

By your acquiring this book, you will be familiarizing yourself with the author's style of writing, specialized (and <u>**exclusive**</u>) Knowledge, his rare Insight, and his ability to eloquently, yet *simply*, share VITALLY **practical** information with clarity, conviction, authority, and compelling interest.

Your exposure to this material will afford you the **confidence** that the author's library of OCPD conquering books will serve you well, and be <u>*more than*</u> well worth your monetary **investment** in acquiring them for personal study and incorporation into your life and that of your beloved one **as a couple**.

With purchase of this collection, you will be well on your way to OCPD **relationship healing** and **deliverance**! Godspeed!

Copyright © 2019

by Mack W. Ethridge

Published by **New Frontier Health Research, Inc.**

All rights reserved. Printed in the United
States of America. Permission granted to quote
brief portions of this book provided due credit
is afforded the author.

Cover design by Mack W. Ethridge

Library of Congress Cataloging-in-Publications
Data, Ethridge, Mack W.

The Relationship Restoring OCPD Fundamentals!

(A ***Vibrant Hope*** and *Escaping* Newsletter Repository)
Complete edition

1st Complete Softback Edition
March 2019

Source Credits: tabular presentations

Unless otherwise stated, the design and structure of all tables, charts, and listings were created by the staff of **New Frontier Health Research, Inc**. The statistical content of all such staff-created illustrative materials were derived from multiple, presumed-to-be, reliable sources.

All figures pertain to the United States of America.

ACKNOWLEDGMENTS

I wish to earnestly and humbly thank the Creator of all for the Guidance and Inspiration provided me to produce the much-needed, increasingly-requested, ground-breaking, self-help style, OCPD recovery books, of which this volume is a very advantageous 'prequel'. And, further, had it not been for the tremendously favorable response to my first book (Escaping Another's OCPD Tyranny) addressed to the 'victim' of another's OCPD behaviors, my subsequent book (OCPD's Only Hope of Psychological Wellness) meant for the OCPD person *herself* (or *himself*) would most surely not have been birthed. May this latter-cited book afford the highly valuable and tremendously gifted person who has OCPD the great encouragement and ample support he or she is entitled to; and may this person find the Insight, Understanding, and Wisdom available to them throughout its pages to heal and set them free.

Table of Contents

Conquering Your OCPD Tendencies

Door to a Brighter Tomorrow! Gift Edition **No. 1**

Detrimental Mindsets of the OCPD Person. Gift Edition **No. 2**

Liberating, Truth-Laden Messages for the OCPD Person. Gift Edition **No. 3**

Liberating, Truth-Laden Messages for the OCPD Person – 2nd Installment, Gift Edition **No. 4**

New Book Announcement! When OCPD Meets the Power of God! Special Announcement Edition **No. 5**

Escaping Another's OCPD Tyranny! – OCPD Monthly Newsletter

Telling Another They Have OCPD. Gift Edition **No. 1**

The Golden Guiding Principle. Gift Edition **No. 2**

Third-Party Approach to OCPD. Gift Edition **No. 3**

How to Deal With an OCPD Person's Personal Appearance Upset. Gift Edition **No. 4**

The Hidden, Yet True Opponent, in Your Encounters with an OCPD Person **Gift Edition No. 5**

The Peril that Must be Recognized and Decisively Acted Upon. Gift Edition **No. 6**

The OCPD Wife and Her *Often* Disastrous Impact upon *Both* the Marriage Relationship and Her Motherly Obligation

Table of Contents – *Con.*

The OCPD Wife and <u>Her</u> *Often* Disastrous Impact upon *Both* the Marriage Relationship and Her Motherly Obligation **(quick view table)**

The OCPD Husband and His *Often* Disastrous Impact upon *Both* the Marriage Relationship and His Fatherly Obligation

The OCPD Husband and <u>His</u> *Often* Disastrous Impact upon *Both* the Marriage Relationship and His Fatherly Obligation **(quick view table)**

<u>Declarations of God's TRUTH *Over* OCPD</u>

    (Reinforcement Cards)

    Power Thoughts to <u>*Overcome*</u> OCPD (10)

    Fostering Accurate Self-Image (10)

    Protecting my Mental Health (10)

    Ensuring Health Through True Thought (10)

    Holding to True Appreciation of Money (10)

    Bettering Home Life Relations (10)

    Valuing Relationships Above All (10)

    Enhancing Work Interactions (10)

    My Invincible Strength Against OCPD (10)

Declarations of God's Truth Over OCPD, The Central Golden Key/**Farewell**

A Personal Letter from the Author

This greatly-needed book is a compilation of *selected* issues of the author's two OCPD newsletter series, **Vibrant Hope** (for the OCPD person) and **Escaping Another's OCPD Tyranny** (for the non-OCPD person), and are intended for both the OCPD person and the non-OCPD person who interacts with them.

This is especially so for **married couples**, **domestic partners**, even romantic boyfriend/girlfriend arrangements. In fact, the majority of my clients come to me precisely because one of the spouses has OCPD, and both are caught up in what is often a 'battleground' of conflict, disharmony, and devastating disillusionment.

Due to these, and similarly vital reasons, this book has been compiled, and is meant to lay the *groundwork* for **both parties in romance** to mentally/emotionally grow by providing **basic knowledge**, **highly practical means** and **methods** of addressing various *initial* (and subsequent) **aspects** of the OCPD challenge and situation.

Everything herein, though not explicitly addressed to romantic couples, has direct bearing upon every couple who struggles with OCPD issues, and provides a **beginning framework** of highly *relevant questions* and *solid answers* to prepare them for the more detailed and sophisticated knowledge and techniques required to become a **master** over the OCPD phenomenon and to neutralize its threat.

In short, these articles provide (1) a **starting approach** to, and (2) a **crucial *'ABC'* understanding** of, OCPD, really a platform from which to launch further study into the means and methods of conquering this formidable foe, all of which are available in the author's numerous other books on OCPD, with the disclosure of how to banish it from lovers'/couples' consciousness and their shared lives.

No effort has been made to rewrite or reformat any individual newsletter/commentary issue, as each stands on its own. But, this in no way detracts from the intended joint aim of this book's contents, which is to **educate the novice**, and **intermediary learner** (*especially* couples), about the *real* issues at stake, often unknown/hidden from those couples who need this life-saving, relationship-restoring, **Truths**, the most. These Guideposts, *if* recognized, then, foreshadow a couple's healing, *at last!*

Sincerely, Mack W. Ethridge, President, NFHR, Inc.

Dedication

This Research Report is dedicated to the *multiple millions* of people in America, and the tens of millions more worldwide: highly capable, conscientious people in all walks of life, who through no fault of their own came into this world seemingly **predisposed** to develop a mostly-at-present, little-known, or seldom recognized, mental illness known as **Obsessive-Compulsive Personality Disorder**. Should you be one such person, I hasten to extend the hand of friendship, along with my genuine respect and admiration for your commitment to living a life of uncompromising excellence, *which is the primary motivation underlying all of your thoughts, speech, and actions*. I, also, want to praise you enthusiastically for your willingness to read and ponder this preliminary book, and with open-mindedness, entertain the possibility it just *may* have a message for you which could be life-liberating. But, of one thing, I am sure. You will be the richer, wiser, and happier for it.

Disclaimer

All instruction or recommendations in this book are not in any fashion to be construed as medical advice, either for physical, psychological, or mental ailments. This research paper is not intended to diagnose the existence of OCPD, nor to prescribe treatment. Nor is it meant to professionally analyze the mental health condition or emotional fitness of the OCPD person. Self-assessment tools and related tables for the OCPD person (if present) are provided <u>*only*</u> to give an overall, general assessment, *likely* to be reflective of their present capacity to interact with society as a whole. But, only a qualified mental health practitioner can say for sure. In short, this book is meant for informational purposes, only. Before putting into practice any of its ideas or concepts, you would be well-advised to consult a certified health professional conversant with these matters. Further, while these principles have proven effective for many individuals, the degree of success any <u>particular</u> OCPD person (or *other* person exhibiting a lessor number of OCPD traits) may attain in utilizing the suggested recommendations is dependent upon a multitude of factors, including, but not limited to: the OCPD person's level of intelligence, psychological state, personal temperament, physical condition, determination to succeed, and skillfulness in application of principles. The author claims no responsibility for the reader's use or misuse of any part of this work.

Author Qualifications

Mack Ethridge is a professional writer/researcher/educator, as well as a life-long psychology major, who has devoted thousands of hours to the study of Obsessive-Compulsive Personality Disorder, and draws upon his *first-hand* observations of this disorder in action. He has pioneered methods and techniques of how the OCPD person may best obtain **Insight** into their disorder, and thereby, pave the road to their recovery.

Not a stranger to the medical field, Mack has edited such prestigious periodicals as *The Journal of Neurosurgery*, of world-wide circulation; as well as such notable publications as *The Comprehensive Survey of Doctorate Recipients*, of The National Academy of Sciences; and, as a career editor, has received multiple commendations and awards. As a skilled communicator, he also wrote and published a world-wide newsletter, *The ABP Monitor*, of multiple thousand subscribers teaching them how to evaluate personal and professional business partnerships with discriminating insight and wisdom. Lastly, Mack has *personally witnessed* the ongoing heartache and trauma of a distant relative suffering from their OCPD disorder, and *experienced* the relationship-crippling characteristics of OCPD behaviors by this distant family member over a period of several years. And through this Research Report, he seeks to equip those OCPD people who suffer from this disorder with the beginning prerequisite knowledge and tools necessary for them to progressively become free of all its detrimental, health-harming, and interpersonal relationship assaulting compulsions; and for the non-OCPD person 'victim', this book will serve to begin to change their 'victim status' to a that of a confident, **invulnerable strongman** or **woman** before the now-useless and ineffectual attacks against their person by the OCPD person !

Mack's first volume on this subject, *Escaping Another's OCPD Tyranny*, is now an international best seller, and he serves as consultant to an ever-growing OCPD clientele. Mack is, also, one of the *few* recognized lay experts in America on this most-distressing personality disorder known as OCPD. His writings on this, and other health-related concerns, are known, and valued, on three continents.

NEW FRONTIER RESEARCH

VIBRANT HOPE ! – CONQUERING OCPD TENDENCIES

INSIGHT! – Your Door to A Brighter Tomorrow!

OCPD's Only Hope of Psychological Wellness!

Acquiring **Insight** to *Transform* Your Life

Gift Edition No. 1

Dear Friend and Courageous Person,

I congratulate you on your recognition that you have (or, at least, admit the *possibility* of having) Obsessive Compulsive Personality Disorder, otherwise known as **OCPD**. This recognition, *alone*, takes a high degree of self-evaluative capacity, objectivity, intelligence, and personal bravery that many OCPD persons do not possess, and regrettably may never acquire. (Reasons why this is so will be explored in later issues.) Some of you have had your mental health professional inform you of their diagnosis of your condition, and probably persuade you of this, which you acknowledged to your admirable credit. Others of you have come to believe (yes, become convinced) you have this disorder through personal research and self-analysis, and personality trait inventory. Either way, you have been graced with a measure of **Insight** which allows you to 'step back from yourself' and view yourself realistically and truthfully. And it is this very capability which will prove wholly instrumental in your life becoming more of an adventure and a fulfilling and enjoyable affair, as opposed to a hurtful, struggle-filled, and problematic one.

The wonderful thing about **Insight** is that by your paying attention to it, pondering and reflecting upon it, *consistently*, it tends to grow, opening the door to further 'revelations' and 'Aha!' moments that will shed an ever-increasing light on those psychological motives and behavioral patterns which are disrupting and diminishing your life, and frequently, even *more so*, the lives of those around you.

And that, my friend, is the entire focus of the 'Only Hope' book which you have purchased. With faithful and <u>habitual</u> reading, reflection, practice, and more practice (don't worry, it will become easier and finally second-nature!), you will begin to 'undue' those mental thought patterns (obsessions) and behavioral activities (compulsions) which have so hindered you from enjoying your life, and prevented you from appreciating those persons around you.

So, what precisely IS '**Insight**'? Insight has to do with the ability to <u>*discern*</u> or <u>*perceive*</u> the Truth of a matter. It involves <u>*grasping*</u> the true nature or **Reality** of a situation. It usually entails careful and accurate analysis or diagnosis of a major interest, problem, difficulty, or challenge. Although, at times, the Truth of a given scenario may be suddenly arrived at through intuition, or a 'flash' of understanding. Either way, **Insight** affords an individual a comprehension that is in total alignment with the Facts of what is *really* transpiring, and makes what is an ill-informed and/or confused matter to others, plain and self-evident to the bearer of **Insight**. In other words, this quality of consciousness enables a person, more so than anything else, to KNOW the Truth, and in KNOWING a given Truth, to be set free by it!

Now, what does it mean to be 'set free through Insightful Truth'?

In the context of OCPD, with every glimmer of insight, each recognition of yours, *to yourself*, of the many ways in which YOU are sabotaging your precious life, creating unhappiness and misery and discontent, that you acknowledge (which is to say, **pause** to become aware of), you become that much more free to discard that false viewpoint and to cease from carrying out detrimental behaviors. It is as though a 'Light' has been turned on, and you are no longer so easily drawn down a path that you can now clearly see (or at least increasingly suspect) as unnecessary, uncalled for, and senseless to pursue relative to truly desirable ends.

For example, let's say you have just come home from work and after greeting your spouse, you notice your loved one has laid a pile of folded bath towels on the kitchen chair. You immediately think to yourself, 'What is he (or she) thinking? Why haven't the towels been taken to the bedroom or bathroom closet? What an oversight!' After which, you automatically, *without thinking*, begin to berate your loved one about their neglect in putting the towels where they belong. This vocal action on your part is not likely to foster harmony or goodwill between the two of you, don't you agree? After all, there may be quite legitimate reasons why the towels were there, such as a brief distraction from a phone call, a visitor, something remembered that needed immediate attention, or even a spell of weakness. But, whatever the reason, wouldn't it be more sensible, and **peace preserving**, to allow the towels to stay there for a while, after which time your spouse will probably move them at a time more opportune for them. No big deal. Nothing has been harmed. Where towels are *temporarily* placed, after all, is really of little consequence or importance. **This, dear friend, is the Truth or the Reality of the matter.** If you genuinely think otherwise, it is because your OCPD tendencies are being activated, and you are losing sound and wholesome perspective.

This, however, is <u>not</u> to say that should the towels be left there for a few days, you do not have the right to ask your spouse to kindly place them where they belong. By all means, **do** ask them should this occur. But, recognize that **demanding** of your loved one to do something the moment you bring it to their attention is immature and even a violation of that person's rights and even their human dignity.

Another example: let's say that you are a passenger in the car your spouse is driving, and you are beginning to become aware (gaining **Insight**) that you often tell your spouse to 'get in the right lane, dear, as you will need to turn soon.' Up to this point, you may not have realized that even though your intention is good, your 'good intention' is creating an irritated driver who well knows he (or she) will need to merge into the right lane, but will do so at a time of their choosing. So, next time you feel inclined to 'remind' your spouse that they should get into the right lane, practice self-control and say nothing. Undoubtedly, this will be difficult for you to do at first, but over time, it will become easier. And, what if your spouse does *not* change lanes in time, and misses the turn? Then, **accept** the fact that she (or he) missed the turn! By you not predictably bringing up the idea that a lane change is overdue, you might be surprised to find that your spouse will eventually learn to change lanes with plenty of time to spare – <u>or they may not</u>! Again, either way, by your *not* speaking and by exercising self-discipline by refraining from telling your spouse what to do, you are allowing them to grow at their own pace, and become a more responsible driver, as well. No harm was done if the turn was missed, after all!

And a final example might be when your brother or sister spends some time with you on their vacation time. This loved one has come over during an extended holiday weekend to spend several nights. But, what they find is that you **insist** upon their taking a shower before they turn in each night, as you feel the bed linens are too fine to have someone sleep in them without showering first. Here, you are attempting to **impose** your standards of cleanliness upon a sibling who probably showered that very morning, and may not need to take a shower at all due to little or no exertion made during the day, in other words, little or no perspiration occurred. Also, your sibling may be accustomed to a simple, but wholly adequate 'wash up' at the bathroom sink, from time to time, when a shower is not practical or a bath really is not called for.

That, dear friend, may sound nonsensical to your present way of thinking, but it is right here that you must come to terms with the Fact that your OCPD mentality is encroaching, *again*, upon you and your loved one. The Truth is <u>many</u> people can go for several days without showering, as long as they wash at the sink, and/or freshen up with any number of cleanliness or bath aids, without exhibiting any body odor whatsoever. It all depends upon a person's bio-individuality, and personal preference. So, restrain yourself from **demanding** a relative's compliance with your strong insistence! If on the other hand, this person truly does exude a strong body odor, then you are *well within your rights* to bring this to their attention, again, tactfully; and you may request, with firmness, that both you and they will be much more at ease and comfortable by their bathing or showering so that they will be fresh and clean. Nothing wrong with that! But, be sure to distinguish the one case from the other! By doing so, you will ensure 'domestic tranquility' and honor each the other.

Actually, so much of all of this pertains to 'natural' sense if recognized and adhered to. Of course, it will take practice to *retrain* your mind to think along more logical, practical, mutually-beneficial interpersonal relationship interactions, but it is well within your power to do so.

Keep your 'Only Hope' workbook close at hand – on your nightstand, on the corner of your desk, in your briefcase, in your automobile while driving, wherever it will be readily available when you need it. Also, photocopy the Reminder/Motivation 'Cards' and keep them on your person for frequent review throughout your day. These, along with the meditations, self-esteem builders, and powerful positive declarations will begin to lessen the grip of OCPD upon you, day by day, and begin to allow you more and more 'breathing spaces' created by your relinquishing of attitudes of demandingness, criticalness, complaining, perfectionistic ways of thinking, and all the other harmful maladaptive and dysfunctional traits enumerated in **Only Hope** for you to become vitally aware of so that you may 'nip their arising in the bud' before they emerge.

You have begun a wholly worthwhile journey! And the outcome will be your liberation from a *tightly constricted* life of worry, unhappiness, discontent, and tormenting fear. You deserve a life of true Freedom! Be a slave to nothing or no one, anymore! Certainly not to any obsessive/compulsive thoughts! And a life of authentic personal Power, increasing Satisfaction with yourself, and vibrant Hope will be yours! Till next time,

Sincere Well Wishes, and Great Belief – in YOU! Mack W. Ethridge

PS: Friends, I would like to add some further closing thoughts on this all-important idea of **Insight** which I feel will be to your benefit. Should you have the opportunity, at some time you might wish to become familiar with a book entitled *I Am Not Sick, I Don't Need Help!* By Dr. Xavier Amador (Available through Amazon online). And be sure it is the 10th anniversary edition, as well. Now, while it is true that you <u>do</u> recognize you are in need of changing the way you think and behave to experience a richer, fuller, more rewarding life (and *I Am Not Sick* speaks to those who <u>don't</u> have this recognition), there is nevertheless much wisdom here you can benefit by. In other words, though you, by the Grace of Life, have a genuine measure of **Insight**, there will undoubtedly be times when the Truth of a situation or circumstance or behavior will escape you. And the consequence will be the three 'D's' of distress, dissatisfaction, and discontent, not to mention disharmony and perhaps even outright conflict with others. That, my friend, is only natural and to be expected.

After all, it is your present **Insight** that will *progressively* lead you into greater Insight relative to the many varied nonproductive and relationship-harming traits of OCPD thinking and behaviors. Stated another way, you will have Insight empowering you to change in some instances, and you will not (initially) possess Insight to change in other instances. The Truth of a given situation will simply 'pass right over your head.' But, over time, with your **Intention** set to uncover your 'blind spots', you WILL experience those flashes of awareness that will inform you of the harmfulness of your thoughts and actions, providing you with strong incentive to alter those thoughts and modify those actions to the benefit of all. In fact, whenever you experience inner upset, or lack of peacefulness, you would do well to pause and consider whether or not you are in the grip of OCPD manifestation. This will allow for **Insight** to 'intervene' and for you to find relief from distress, and for you to grow.

So, in closing, dear friend, know that **YOU** actually <u>**DO**</u> possess the **Power within** you to alter your life for the better through your **commitment** to do so. OCPD, admittedly, is a formidable challenge, requiring deep soul-searching, a fearless honesty with yourself, and a <u>*ruthless*</u> scrutiny and analysis of those thoughts you entertain in your mind, on a recurring basis. It requires **training** your mind to recognize and to _abandon_ erroneous, detrimental, contrary-to-reality thoughts (and their associated hurtful and life-diminishing feelings) and to **embrace** accurate, mental-health engendering, _faithful_-to-reality thoughts that will support you, strengthen, you, and cause you to – in a wonderfully freeing and beautiful state of psychological freedom – to TRULY LIVE!

In other words, the training will require a **heart-held dedication** to meet OCPD head-on, but _never_ doubt for one moment that you can CONQUER it! I am here to tell you with all the fiber of my being that YOU CAN! In Truth, you WILL become the MASTER over OCPD, in time. I believe you are destined to do so! For, Life does NOT allow you to undergo difficult times without equipping you with the capacity to OVERCOME those difficulties! In fact, it is in the overcoming of it, that you will be the **better** for it! This is a Universal Law of Life!

Also, continue to remind yourself that you ARE a being of extraordinary Worth and Value, one who is deserving of experiencing a life of _enjoyment, satisfaction, fulfillment, well-being, inner peace, gratifying purpose, and rewarding accomplishment_, regardless as to the demerits of your past beliefs, speech, actions, or behaviors. You have done the best you knew how at the time. You are a child of the Universe, a son or daughter of Life, **Itself**! You are on a NEW PATH now! You are on the Road – _to Victory_!

With firm belief in you, and in your **Vibrant Mental Health** to come, I remain your supporter and, I pray, worthy helper. Sincerely, _Mack W. Ethridge_

DISCLAIMER: No recommendations within this newsletter are to be construed as medical advice, but only as educational reference material. Embarking upon any psychological or bodily health venture should be discussed with and overseen by one's personal mental health practitioner or physician. Author disavows all responsibility for use or misuse by newsletter recipient, or their loved ones, of research material herein.

NEW FRONTIER RESEARCH

VIBRANT HOPE ! – CONQUERING OCPD TENDENCIES

The Many Detrimental Mindsets of the OCPD Person

OCPD's Only Hope of Psychological Wellness!

Acquiring **Insight** to *Transform* Your Life

Gift Edition No. 2

Dear Friend and Courageous Person,

Please bear in mind that the following characteristics belong to the person who has *full-blown* OCPD. That is, this person possesses these dysfunctional traits to a *severe* and *maximal* degree. These dear people who are wholly 'possessed' by the OCPD mentality have 'zero' amount of **Insight**, which regrettably, consigns them to the world of the incurable – apart from a Divine Intervention from God.

ut, should you, who are reading this newsletter possess a modicum (or miniscule amount) of **Insight**, allowing you to see yourself with accuracy, objectivity, and detachment, that alone, there is yet <u>considerable</u> hope for you to break free from the shackles OCPD which now so limit and diminish and distress your precious life. do not despair! And your reading of this newsletter commentary, and as well, also proves you are one of the fortunate ones who have **Awareness** (another name for **Insight**), which when consciously cultivated will grow into liberating attitudes, dispositions, and mindsets. And, again, just what is **Insight**? It is that all-important faculty or capability of discerning the true nature or operation of a situation, process, or a person – what is *really* transpiring in any given arena.

The following five mindsets are some of the more prominent detrimental mindsets that even the OCPD person <u>WITH</u> Insight may exhibit and be subject to IF they are not careful, and IF they do not monitor their thoughts (and feelings), and analyze and evaluate them for falsity, departure from reality, and the negative consequences such thoughts will inevitably generate.

Harmful Mindset No. 1 – An Unteachable Spirit

Far too often, the OCPD person unfortunately can only be described as **'unteachable'**. This characteristic derives from their utter obstinacy, or stubbornness, to believe others have anything of value or truthfulness or even trustworthiness to teach them for their benefit – this in spite of overwhelming evidence to the contrary! – disclosing their irrationality, lack of logic, and immature (undeveloped) thinking processes, patterns and perceptual interpretations. The OCPD person (again, the one with the <u>*full-blown*</u> traits) sincerely believes that they 'know it all' and that they are essentially 'smarter than all others'.

...tly whether they actually believed this, they ...ew wouldn't!), but their habitual speech and ...ooftops! What they don't realize, don't even ...t they are being 'host' to (or you could say, ...human ego that would exalt itself over its ...in an egotistical way, frequently with ... Yet, even here, this OCPD-possessed ego can ...itself, with soft speech and slow, almost ...ions, as well, which only proves her or his ...on of and disregard for another's instruction, wise ...ions, counsel, or proffered knowledge. Knowledge that is ...nsidered may well prove to be a tremendous blessing to the OCPD person *if only* they would give it a fair trial in their lives.

So, if you have OCPD, but by God's Grace, you possess a measure of **Insight**, then remain conscious (remind yourself) of the fact that you, in all likelihood, have a <u>*propensity to be unteachable*</u>, and that by recalling this harmful trait to mind, you can 'nip it in the bud' when it seeks to 'rear its ugly head' into your thinking and feeling worlds.

Harmful Mindset No. 2 – Readiness to Reject Answers and Solutions

This harmful mindset correlates with the unteachable mindset in that if you are unteachable, then you most certainly will be **rejecting sound, viable, answers – and practical, workable solutions to your problems and difficulties,** as a matter of course. Whether those problems be physical, mental, financial, relational, occupational, or spiritual. My beloved relative, who has OCPD, and with whom I interact daily (we live in the same house), consistently and *predictably*, (and yes, sorrowfully, to me) routinely jettisons answers and solutions offered to her by her medical practitioner, other professional (highly knowledgeable) guides

and counselors, and by myself who am her concerned [...]
only desires to help her. My beloved relative NEVER is will[...]
possible solution or remedy a *try*, even for the briefest perio[...]
and consequently never reaps the benefit of the many remedies [...]
exist to most any problem or challenge in her world. How blind such
people are to what they are doing to themselves!

So, if you have OCPD but are **Insightful** to even a modest degree, you
have within your hands the capability of *self-observation*, wherein you
can detect this likely predisposition of yours to reject answers and
solutions, and in recognizing it can combat it, and *override* it, to adopt
various possible remedies to your problems, and give them that 'good ol'
college try', which more often than not will yield, at some point, partial, if
not total success. The watchword is: **Be willing to try!** – New things!
Different things! Even Unlikely things! Even things you are *dis-inclined* to
try. Those may be the very answers and solutions you seek!

Harmful Mindset No. 3 – Refusal to Self-Reflect

The OCPD person who is totally possessed by the OCPD syndrome (this
constellation of harmful traits) may *momentarily* 'reflect' upon any given
positive or hopeful suggestions offered by another, but very quickly
ceases doing so, as the longer they do, the greater their anxiety becomes,
as it becomes more clear to them that they (the OCPD person herself or
himself) are mistaken, or wrong. And the thought of being wrong is
unbearable to them! So, they often say, 'I don't want to think about it.'

Therefore self-examination, self-observation, or self-reflection – *relative
to their openness to an idea* – is something the OCPD person seldom will
consent to doing. It simply is too unsettling to them, so this person simply
refuses to endure the momentary discomfort, and instead, adheres to
their 'default' (or automatic) position of 'I'm right, you're wrong', or 'your
solution can't possibly work because I was not the one to think of it, *first*'.

...ut **can** see through the fallacy of refusing to self-
... good sense or sound judgment) upon your
... hen you can adopt another's suggestions as your
... hose suggestions into your daily activities to prove
... validity. Should they prove to be non-solutions,
... hem and try something else.

... remain unwilling to *try* different approaches, various techniques, or alternate ways of doing things, you will most certainly never resolve your problems, nor will you meet any of your challenges successfully. That is a given. And should be a wake-up call to anyone – with OCPD, or not.

Harmful Mindset No. 4 – Insistence Upon Circular Thoughts and Cyclical Conversation

The OCPD person with full-blown OCPD has the very entrenched, disquieting and discouraging habit (to them and those around them) of either mentally or orally **rehearsing a problem *over* and *over* again – focusing upon the problem, instead of taking ACTION and initiating possible solutions**. Apparently, the OCPD person never developed personal initiative, self-starting behaviors, and motive power. And, what is worse, such a person exhibits absolutely <u>no</u> desire to acquire these life-enhancing attributes. Their expressed thoughts consist of unending 'loops' (to use computer language), going around and around in circles – always ending up where they started with <u>no</u> perceived options, <u>no</u> possible answers, and <u>no</u> probable solutions. In fact, the OCPD person is afraid of trying ANYTHING out of fear of failing and appearing incompetent and incapable. So, such a person just ruminates, or mulls, over a problem and how they suffer from it without seeking a way out. An example would be: 'I hate it when I have no suitable table to place in that corner of the house. That corner looks so vacant, so empty. The vase sitting there on the floor just doesn't 'cut it'! If only there were one there. But I don't have one. It is just such a pity. Every time I look in that direction I get upset. I know I am going to be unhappy all day because of that. I hate it! I hate It!' – And on and on it goes without any thought that there surely would be a suitable table in the garage, stored in the attic, one that can be obtained inexpensively at a yard sale, or purchased from a local department store. The bemoaning is repeated day after day. But, if you suggest any of the above alternatives to the vase, you get a reply such as: 'No, I don't have the time for that now', or 'No, there would be too many spider webs on the table in the attic.' Or 'No, it would take too long to drive to the department store and probably would be a waste of gasoline.' Etcetera, etcetera!

You, on the other hand, who possess some **Insight** realize you may have this tendency to complain, and bemoan, and despair. But in your case, you can catch yourself before you do so, or at the very least discontinue those behaviors shortly after they start. Become sensitive to *how* you are hurting yourself, and <u>vow</u> to break this mental trap that colors your day with unproductiveness and negativity.

Harmful Mindset No. 5 – Detecting Others' Faults Without Realizing They Possess the *Identical* Faults

The OCPD person, particularly the one with full-blown symptoms, is a master at <u>clearly</u> seeing any number of character faults in their fellow-woman and -man, but are oblivious to the fact that they possess the same fault, more often than not, in a much more *pronounced* way. This is blindness to the ultimate degree! Such dear OCPD people will say, 'How can *they* be so blind as to what is going on?', or 'How is it that *they* cannot see what *they* are doing that is driving people away from them?', or 'Don't *they* realize they are creating their own troubles?', and the like.

So, if the OCPD person who is only moderately (yet, still very *problematically*) OCPD, has a measure of **Insight**, he or she can become cognizant of their tendency to make remarks about others in this fashion, and can begin to curtail such talk. All the while, turning the spotlight of their own inner consciousness toward their OCPD selves with the aim of recognizing their harmful speech and hurtful interpersonal relationship behaviors. It all comes back to self-awareness, or conscious awareness of the <u>nature</u> of their OCPD thoughts and speech patterns, what lies behind those thoughts, and the undesirable consequences that invariably result.

Friend, become a person who studies yourself! Accept the fact that as an OCPD person you need to become *acutely aware* of your urges to speak and act in certain undesirable ways. The path to freedom lies therein!

Till next time,

Sincere Well Wishes,

Mack W. Ethridge

DISCLAIMER: No recommendations within this newsletter are to be construed as medical advice, but only as educational reference material. Embarking upon any psychological or bodily health venture should be discussed with and overseen by one's personal mental health practitioner or physician. Author disavows all responsibility for use or misuse by newsletter recipient, or their loved ones, of research material herein.

NEW FRONTIER RESEARCH

VIBRANT HOPE ! – CONQUERING OCPD TENDENCIES

Liberating Truth-Laden Messages for the OCPD Person

OCPD's Only Hope of Psychological Wellness!

Acquiring **Insight** to *Transform* Your Life

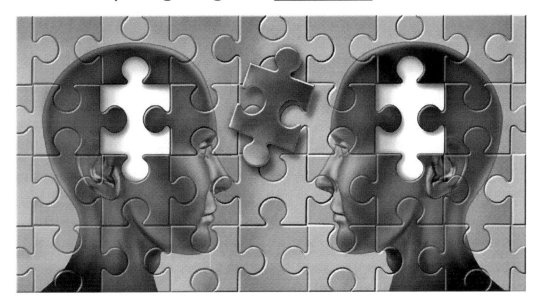

Gift Edition No. 3

Dear Friend and Courageous Person,

This edition of Vibrant Hope truly contains compact, psychologically-sound – and **powerful**, Truth-laden Messages, which through consistent reflection upon and reciting, will serve to 'renew your mind', and **cause** you to become *ever-the-more* aware of **Life's Great Laws** governing your human relations and your happiness. Your application of them will, with all assurance, transform your life into one of harmony, cooperation, and joy, as you use them in conjunction with *OCPD's Only Hope of Psychological Wellness* guide and workbook.

To start with, your approach to your OCPD condition has everything to do with how successful you will be in conquering those traits and characteristics that trouble you so. First and foremost, you need to be told **The Truth** that though the battle will be strenuous, <u>at times</u>, **YOU** have it <u>well within your power</u> to be the **VICTOR** over this condition that would so diminish the quality of your life, and would harm your precious personal relationships.

This is encouraging and wonderful news!

So read on and adopt the <u>confident</u> mental viewpoint that will enable you to approach any OCPD situation with a spirit of **authority** and victory, as you <u>internalize</u> the mindset that will, eventually, give you mastery over a condition you WILL one day view as something of your long-ago past, alone! Let's begin!

Power Thoughts to <u>*Overcome*</u> OCPD

1. I am **convinced** it is entirely possible for me to overcome my OCPD tendencies in a relatively *short* period of time. And, I realize I have **compelling reasons** to do so. I recognize that I have what it takes to succeed. And I <u>**WILL**</u> succeed!

2. I am making the **conscious decision**, right now, to become **free** from OCPD urges. I <u>accept</u> this view as my Destiny! I **resolutely declare** myself to be OCPD free <u>now</u>! And I **commit** myself to this ideal. I will be <u>consistent</u> in my application of **True Thought**.

3. I will tell myself the **TRUTH** that I am _wholly_ _deserving_ of becoming free from OCPD. And that this Goal, _once achieved_, will be a **blessing** and a noble aim. My Success is a **foregone conclusion** and is _NOT_ open to debate! I need only _persevere_ to win!

4. I _genuinely_ and _strongly_ **desire** to be set free from OCPD shackles. I, here and now, **claim** vibrant mental health as my natural **birthright**! I declare I am a **_Rightful Heir_** to a sound mind. And I **Vow** to persist in monitoring my thoughts _till_ I achieve my freedom.

5. In the depths of my being, I **Invoke** the **Spirit** of **Victory**. I recognize the time has come for my **deliverance** from OCPD to take place. I acknowledge _my duty to myself_ to achieve this worthy Goal of mental healthfulness, and I am **committed** to _becoming free_!

6. The looked-forward-to, resultant **Joy** of living in a continual state of **mental health**, _free from OCPD tendencies_, serves to _greatly_ **motivate** me to become _ever-the-more_-mindful of the **quality** of my thoughts. I can and **WILL** become far more happy by doing so.

7. I now choose to be **bold** in declaring that I will _no longer_ tolerate OCPD characteristics. In fact, I **decree** with **absolute conviction** and **perfect certainty** that Success **WILL** be mine! It simply is _not_ possible that I can fail due to the **strength** of my unconquerable desire, and my **committed determination** to persevere.

8. I was _born_ with the **Innate Power** to _eliminate_ my OCPD foe. I **dare** believe this is so, because it _IS_ so! Therefore, I will act in behalf of

my **best interests**, Trusting my **God-given ability** to _master_ this foe! I know my commitment _will_ overcome **all** obstacles.

9. I am **persuaded** that the life I desire, _free from all_ OCPD hindrances and obsessions, not to mention, compulsions, is **attainable**. I will _no longer_ believe it cannot be done. It **CAN** be done, and I am DOING it! I **CAN** change, and I **AM** changing, _becoming free!_

10.   I will procure _whatever_ product or service available to me **proven** to equip people to _vanquish_ their OCPD foe. I will record my progress in a **journal**. I remind myself that seemingly 'small' Victories are _stepping stones_ to **Big** success! I will _review_ these concepts daily.

So there you have, dear friend, the mental stance that is **necessary** for you to _come to believe_ as wholly true, _if_ you are to achieve the wellness and deliverance you seek and are so deserving of as a beloved child of Life and the Universe. Yes, you may not believe _all_ of the above at this time, but you CAN **come to believe** it as you tell yourself, each day, that the above Truth Proclamations are _SO!_

Therefore, commit to reading and reciting these statements _every_ day at least once. At the very beginning of your day is preferable as it is then that you set the tone for your day, which tends to positively 'color' whatever you think, say, or do. Or, should you find any particular statements as 'speaking to you' more so than others, by all means, focus on them – the most.

But, whatever you do, do _not_ discount the **power** that is inherent in these Truth Statements! They are a **MAJOR key** to your becoming free!

And lastly, here are further thoughts to hasten your deliverance:

Protecting my Mental Health

1. Today, I will experience the **many benefits** of **mental health** ideals and practices when interacting with my fellow-woman and -man. This means I will extend to them a **highly respectful** stance regarding _their_ autonomy and their obligation to exercise it.

2. To be **mentally healthy** is surely the greatest blessing one can have in life. It is a **prize** worth my fighting for, and a nourishing _environment_ to be pursued. Even physical health cannot be compared to it. _For **mental health** will afford me **Peace**, or _True_ Power!_

3. To be **mentally healthy** is to be _clear_ in my view of myself, and _strong_ in my conviction of its _accuracy_. To know that my mind can be, and **IS**, a citadel of strength when **I take conscious possession** of its vast powers for good in **upholding** _others'_ dignity with grace.

4. The possession of **mental health** will safeguard my _emotional_ world, keep me **balanced** in outlook, and **calm** in intention. I _no longer_ need self-create and experience turmoil _by clinging to fallacious ideas of life_ as being dreadful and not worth living.

5. To be _continually_ critical of others is a **direct attack** upon another's well-being and mental composure, whether my criticism is justified, or _not_. This is a crucial concept to understand, as **grasping** it will **free me** from the prison of its poison circulating through my life!

6. I take time, today, to salute whatever guardian there may be of **mental health**. For some, there is a _patron saint_ who oversees this domain. For others, the **Living God**. But, I hail such a one for promoting its expansion in my mind, and give thanks for its sponsorship.

7. By looking on the **bright side** of things, I am <u>proclaiming</u> to Life that I **trust** It, and *believe* It is wholly on my side as a **son** or **daughter** of Its heart. So though I don't <u>yet</u> see the **full picture** of any given situation, I can **rest assured** there is behind everything an **ultimate** good.

8. An important aspect of <u>*protective*</u> **mental health** is the firm conviction that I possess *more than enough* power to confront any <u>disappointment</u> with equanimity and an **undisturbed state** of mind. This includes when others fall short of <u>*my*</u> expectations.

9. I choose to adopt, <u>today</u>, sound, constructive, **mental health** viewpoints, outlooks, and practices so that I might <u>*thoroughly enjoy my life*</u>, and be **an enjoyment** to all others I meet. My 'giving up' complaining is **a big part** of the remedy, which I gladly do.

10. To live as though others are **fully capable** of <u>*self-determination*</u>, apart from <u>my</u> unwanted interference, is a **life-enhancing** creed which serves <u>*me*</u> well. Others <u>will</u> make mistakes, and fail. But, this is all a part of the learning process designed for our highest good.

Till next time,

Sincere Well Wishes,

Mack W. Ethridge

PS: **Fostering Accurate Self-Image** will be explored next month! God bless!

DISCLAIMER: No recommendations within this newsletter are to be construed as medical advice, but only as educational reference material. Embarking upon any psychological or bodily health venture should be discussed with and overseen by one's personal mental health practitioner or physician. Author disavows all responsibility for use or misuse by newsletter recipient, or their loved ones, of research material herein.

NEW FRONTIER RESEARCH

VIBRANT HOPE ! – CONQUERING OCPD TENDENCIES

Liberating Truth-Laden Messages for the OCPD Person – <u>2</u>*nd Installment.*

OCPD's Only Hope of Psychological Wellness!

Acquiring **Insight** to *Transform* Your Life

Gift Edition No. 4

Dear Friend and Courageous Person,

This edition of Vibrant Hope continues the theme of psychologically-sound – and **powerful**, Truth-laden Messages, begun last month, which through consistent reflection upon and reciting, will serve to 'renew your mind', and **cause** you to become *ever-the-more* aware of **Life's Great**

Laws governing your human relations and your happiness. And as stated before, your application of them will, with all assurance, transform your life into one of harmony, cooperation, and joy, as you use them in conjunction with *OCPD's Only Hope of Psychological Wellness* guide and workbook.

So we will pick up where we left off and adopt the <u>confident</u> mental viewpoint that will enable you to approach any OCPD situation with a spirit of **authority** and **victory**, as you <u>internalize</u> the mindset that will, eventually, give you mastery over a condition you WILL one day view as something of your long-ago past, alone! We resume with:

Fostering Accurate Self-Image

11. I can feel <u>*utterly*</u> safe and <u>*wholly*</u> secure in knowing that others' talents and gifts are *not* a threat to me. In fact, I can **rejoice** in their good fortune, and I do! I **renounce** the errant thought that I am <u>diminished</u> in their presence, and instead feel **great pride** in them.

12. My **self-perception** has everything to do with my level of *life satisfaction*. I can know that I am **as good** as the next person, irrespective of my accomplishments or lack thereof. I am **valuable** for no other reason than I'm human, with unique **strengths** and **gifts** to share.

13. Perfection actually lies within me and all about me, *if* I only have 'wits' enough to perceive it. **I AM a *perfectly* imperfect person!** <u>*Seeming*</u> imperfection harbors a vital purpose and serves to **highlight** the **perfection** of my God-Like power <u>*to accept*</u>.

14. I need <u>never</u> doubt my worthiness to live life with **confidence** and **self-assurance**, because I am the **equal** to anyone and *everyone*. Not in terms of talents, to be sure, but in terms of **human dignity** and **rights**. And because of this, I can treat **all** accordingly!

15. I can *legitimately* only **stand tall** among my fellow humans when I afford to them <u>every</u> human courtesy and <u>every</u> consideration I would **demand** for myself. <u>*And this is how it shall be*</u>. To do otherwise is to **stand <u>small</u>** in a world where my self-image is distorted.

16. If I perceive my <u>role</u> in life as one who is <u>*entrusted*</u> with criticizing, blaming, and generally demoralizing others, then I see myself **falsely**. My self-image is flawed, and is <u>*not*</u> in accord with **Reality**. Instead, I shall view myself as a **helper** and as a **defender** of life.

17. *If* I believe myself to be **worthy** of life only *if* I perform '<u>perfectly</u>', then I am misguided, and *self*-deceived. Never will I attain unto a **healthy self-image**, nor will I be able to appreciate <u>*just how wonderful*</u> I truly Am. I, therefore, **renounce** falsehoods of outward perfection.

18. A strong, healthy self-image is one wherein I **relinquish** *past hurts* and disappointments, and **forego** *future anxieties* and <u>*self*</u>-manufactured fears. And because my **Great** Mind is **ONLY** <u>worthy</u> of '<u>*Grand pursuits*</u>', I am <u>un</u>worthy of '*trivial pursuits*' – and wholly capable of **discarding** and living *above* them!

19. It is utter foolishness to believe I have to make another feel *badly* or *inadequate* for me to feel **good** about myself and **all-sufficient**. Any inclination I detect in myself to do this, I <u>ruthlessly</u> 'exorcise' from my psyche and **expel** it! – *I'll have no part in it!*

20. There is no need for me to <u>*inflate*</u> my self-image through **exaggerating** my qualities and **exalting** my capabilities above others. I can <u>honestly</u> and <u>forthrightly</u> and <u>proudly</u> **declare** who **I AM**, without any sense of shame or embarrassment or fear! And **I will**!

Ensuring Health Through True Thought

1. I can become a dynamo of **physical vibrancy** to an <u>*ever*</u>-increasing degree as I <u>one</u>-<u>by</u>-<u>one</u> let go of anger, attempts to control, criticism, complaining, judging, perfectionism, and useless worry. For with **physical stamina** and bodily **strength**, I can <u>*optimally*</u> function.

2. How **wonderful** it is to know that the many health issues I endure can be dealt with <u>*successfully*</u>, often, with **True Thought** alone! Thought IS the 'Master Builder' as scientific research repeatedly confirms. That means, I am in control to a **large extent** of my welfare.

3. Subscribing to **accurate thinking** about my <u>*proper*</u> role in life, and how I can **best** relate to others, *is what overcoming OCPD traits are all about*. Headaches, neck pain, back trouble, digestive upset, even skin and muscle problems <u>often</u> are resolved by **thinking true**.

4. I have at long last learned the **advisability** to think on 'whatsoever is **true**, honest, **just**, pure, lovely, of **good report**, virtue, and

praise'. For by doing so, I erect a powerful _energetic force field_ all about me that promotes vibrant, robust, youthful **health**.

5. I am **done** with aggravating _myself_ at every disappointment my OCPD tendencies have **magnified** all _out of proportion_ to any given action or event. I let all such _over_-reactions go, and hold to _appropriate_ reactions which **preserve** my health and well-being.

6. The Mind-Body Connection is now a proven Reality. With _every_ **positive thought** I am promoting a stronger, healthier body. This is a proven **scientific** FACT! The more _distorted_ OCPD thoughts I challenge and **discard**, the _more_ healthier – and energetic I become.

7. The emotional upset and bodily nervousness I have been so prone to experience while **captive** to the outpicturing of OCPD traits, I can actually now **forestall** and even _eliminate_. My mind controls my body, and here is where control is **warranted** and desired.

8. The mental and **physical fatigue** I routinely experienced while under the sway of OCPD traits, are now _receding_ into the past! **Unburdened** by the heavy load of _false responsibility_ in taking on the burdens of the world has **freed me** to help more _intelligently_.

9. Modern medical science has confirmed that dwelling upon the **positive side** of life experiences **creates an environment** where physical health will _best_ flourish. University studies one after another have verified this **central fact**. I now **choose** to make use of it.

10. My body is continually **outpicturing** the state of my mind. If I want an untroubled and **pain-free** body, I must _encourage_ and _cultivate_ an untroubled and **pain-free** mind. Therefore, I will make _every_ effort today to do just that, and **reap the rewards** thereby.

Valuing Relationships Above All

1. I set my intention, today, to account the **quality** of my relationships as more important than winning arguments, offering unsolicited advice, or verbally 'correcting' supposed mistakes of others. I **resist** these compulsions by seeing 'through' them to their harmfulness.

2. I recognize, at last, the advisability of allowing other people **their right** to make mistakes, the freedom to try things their _own_ way, the personal liberty to experiment as _they_ see fit. As **I would most certainly want** the same consideration extended to me.

3. I now carefully, with pleasure, observe that by adhering to a philosophy of individual personal freedom by **all people** to choose _their_ own way, I am set free _not_ to be **bound** to the distressing role of dictator, superior officer, or task master. **I can be free!**

4. I now **wholeheartedly subscribe** to the empowering belief that the doctrine of political, religious, and economic freedom, _for which so many people have fought and died_, extends to the realm of _interpersonal_ _relationship_ freedom. And serves **just as well**.

5. I now understand that it is _not_ required, _nor_ necessary for me, _nor_ even desirable to, **insist** that others heed _my_ admonitions, _my_

cautions, or *my* 'wise advice'. What works for me may well not work for others – emotionally, or 'energetically'. **This I accept.**

6. I now know that harmonious, cooperative, **satisfying** relationships are highly desirable above any *lessor* desires to control or 'manage' another, which can only damage friendships and/or work relations. Therefore, I wisely choose to relinquish *lessor* desires.

7. I am *so* fortunate to now **know** that I can be *relaxed*, and *feel at peace* while observing another person perform a given task or function in a way **I** would *not* choose to. That is ALL right! **All** are **entitled** to the prerogative of personal choice, even as I.

8. I now *genuinely* believe the **liberating Truth** that honoring another's **personal preference** is **at the same time** honoring my own. No matter that I find *their* preference dissimilar to my own. They are *not* me, *nor* am I them. *Their* preference may precisely fit **their** need.

9. I wisely choose to be ever **vigilant** and **mindful** of any tendency of mine to *usurp* the God-given rights of my fellow-woman and -man to govern their *own* lives independent of my preference, otherwise. I do *not* wish to find myself *in* opposition *to* God's Will.

10. I now fully comprehend I *cannot* expect **fulfilling** relationships with others *if* I **demand** of others to **conform** to *my* way of thinking, doing, acting, or being. All are individuals. *Each* (thankfully) sees things differently. To expect otherwise is foolhardy and naïve.

That concludes the subject matter for this issue.

And as was encouraged before, commit to reading and reciting these statements _every_ day at least once. At the very beginning of your day is preferable as it is then that you set the tone for your day, which tends to positively 'color' whatever you think, say, or do. Or, should you find any particular statements as 'speaking to you' more so than others, by all means, focus on them – the most.

But, whatever you do, do _not_ discount the **power** that is inherent in these Truth Statements! They truly are **MAJOR keys** to your becoming free!

Till next time,

Sincere Well Wishes,

Mack W. Ethridge

PS: **Bettering Home Life** will begin our exploration next month! God bless!

DISCLAIMER: No recommendations within this newsletter are to be construed as medical advice, but only as educational reference material. Embarking upon any psychological or bodily health venture should be discussed with and overseen by one's personal mental health practitioner or physician. Author disavows all responsibility for use or misuse by newsletter recipient, or their loved ones, of research material herein.

NEW FRONTIER RESEARCH

VIBRANT HOPE ! – CONQUERING OCPD TENDENCIES

New Book Announcement!

When OCPD Meets the Power of God!

OCPD's Only Hope of Psychological Wellness!

Acquiring **Insight** to *Transform* Your Life

Special Announcement Edition, March 2015

Dear Friend and Courageous Person,

This edition of Vibrant Hope is being sent to you to inform you of the Author's upcoming *new* book entitled:

'When OCPD Meets the Power of God

– How Insight from Above Will Unlock the Shackles of OCPD Torment and Fear'.

How This Book *Differs* from the Author's Previous Book on OCPD

This book, **When OCPD Meets the Power of God**, will be found to be a refreshingly unique contribution to the field of OCPD observation, study, and discovery; as it offers perspectives <u>*fundamentally*</u> different from the author's former work (addressed directly to the OCPD sufferer) entitled ***OCPD's Only Hope of Psychological Wellness***. This present literary research paper is written with both the OCPD sufferer in mind, as well as the <u>*non*</u>-OCPD person who interacts with the OCPD person.

This work approaches the subject of the mental illness of Obsessive-Compulsive Personality Disorder from the viewpoint of the realm of invisible Spirit – *taking into account the originating Sources of either helpful Insight or harmful influence therefrom, whether for Good or for ill.* While each book presents information and knowledge that is indispensable to the OCPD person if they ever hope to regain, or acquire, their mental and emotional wellness, the latter publication cited above focusses upon the **psychological** aspects, whereas this newly-released publication concentrates principally upon the **spiritual** aspects.

That is why <u>both</u> books come highly recommended to the reader as they complement each other to a 'tee', and serve to reinforce each other in a dovetail fashion. So though it is true that OCPD people are being healed and liberated from OCPD slavery through their conscientious study of **OCPD's Only Hope**, and their consistent application of the principles, techniques, and special knowledge provided therein (thanks be to God!), there almost certainly will be some instances where <u>*only*</u> the knowledge provided in **When OCPD Meets <u>the</u> <u>Power</u> <u>of</u> <u>God</u>**, and the faithful application of that knowledge, will be the catalyst for a more speedy and permanent deliverance, at last.

In short, **Insight** is investigated to a depth never before done, relative to its exact nature, its presence or absence, blocks to its entrance, sources of its coming, what *inhibits* its emergence, or *what allows it to flourish*. The answers may surprise you, but it is *The* Truth that will set men free!

Text for back cover of new book

It is unanimously recognized by psychologists, therapists, and mental health practitioners, alike, that the highly distressing, life-diminishing, and relationship destroying characteristics of Obsessive Compulsive Personality Disorder can be overcome by the acquiring of that elusive 'thing' called INSIGHT. Yet, the question remains: 'How CAN such understanding be gained by the OCPD person who, by nature, is resistant to all change and new ways of thinking in the first place? Come with the author to learn precisely HOW this can be done through the use of a host of experimentally-validated, and *spiritually*-proven techniques that stretch back thousands of years. Learn what the 'most learned', even the skilled researchers, do not know about OCPD due to THEIR lack of Insight relative to the vital mental/spiritual component they either disbelieve or deny. And, then, should an OCPD person grasp these 'revelatory' concepts (this book will show them how), their life can begin to be transformed from one of self-created misery and discontent (a terror to be around!), to a life of joyfulness, satisfaction, and profound fulfillment. Simply put, this book reveals the SOURCE of all Insight, and the ways to open one's self to receiving Its Illuminating, person-freeing Truths! Know, too, these 'teachings' are wholly in keeping with sound psychological practices and principles, offering bright-shining Hope and Certain Help when the OCPD person is in need! While deliverance, should he or she choose (and God willing) WILL follow!

'We cannot be truly sane without being connected to our deeper Self and to God,' by Mark Foley, O.C.D., author, lecturer, and retreat leader

Little Known Facts about Author

Mack Ethridge is uniquely qualified as no other person alive today to author '**When OCPD Meets the Power of God!**' as he is America's premier OCPD lay expert, having written the world's first and *only* comprehensive textbook and original, innovative workbooks on Obsessive Compulsive Personality Disorder, supplying his best-selling treatment and recovery volumes to the North Shore/Long Island Health Care System in New York; and he is also a leading expert on little-known, also new and restored, specialized aspects of Biblical knowledge (concerning our astounding Identity in Christ, claiming our Freedom in Christ, exercising our Authority in Christ, and, perhaps most importantly, obtaining the Deliverance available through Christ, at every level of our beings, including mental/emotional/psychological, as well as spiritual); whose books are in the private libraries of such world notables as Professor N.T. Wright, Andy Andrews, Claire Pfann, Marilla Ness, Akiane Kramarik, Tony Robbins, and Pastor Joel Osteen. And he heads the Mercy Rose Ministries Worldwide Outreach, in operation, now, for nine years, as its Founder and Operational Director.

And with profound, scholarly Insights into the psychological makeup and inner motivations of OCPD people, arrived at through *thousands of hours*, spanning a number of years, of research, ongoing direct, intimate contact, interaction with, and keen observation of OCPD persons, and Mack's intensive decades-long heart search into the spiritual depths of authentic Biblical Christianity, Mack stands wholly unequalled among OCPD researchers, writers, and instructors, as well as clearly unmatched among Christian ministers, teachers, and counselors, in his ability to convey Vital, life-freeing practices, disciplines, and Truths to OCPD people in the capacity of Master Teacher and Christian Scholar/Counselor, par excellence! This one-of-a-kind psycho-spiritual combination of knowledge, skills, and heavenly communication gift of Mack's, so expertly synthesized, has produced a volume destined to become a trailblazing classic in the annals of OCPD Hope for Healing messages and Practices, and Illuminated Philosophy, for the OCPD person to safeguard and preserve their new-found, or rather newly-*bestowed* Freedom and Deliverance, and <u>Victory</u>, from Above – <u>at</u> <u>long</u> <u>last</u>! – *by New Frontier Staff*

I do hope all of you are growing in your knowledge and practice of OCPD overcoming methods and techniques. If you have not had *significant* success, to date, I encourage you to <u>keep</u> studying, <u>continue</u> learning, and <u>persistently</u> practice. And, of course, avail yourself of whatever psychological counseling you feel may be of help to you. You're in my prayers.

Till next time,

  In God's love,

    – And Sincere Well Wishes!

Mack W. Ethridge

President of New Frontier Health Research

    and Director of Mercy Rose Ministries, Intl.

PS: The normal theme trend will continue next month.

DISCLAIMER: No recommendations within this newsletter are to be construed as medical advice, but only as educational reference material. Embarking upon any psychological or bodily health venture should be discussed with and overseen by one's personal mental health practitioner or physician. Author disavows all responsibility for use or misuse by newsletter recipient, or their loved ones, of research material herein.

NEW FRONTIER RESEARCH

OCPD MONTHLY NEWSLETTER

Telling *Another* They Have OCPD

Escaping Another's OCPD Tyranny!

Solving the Puzzle

Gift Edition No. 1

Dear Friend and Fellow Journeyer,

The question that loved ones, friends, and concerned associates of OCPD people often ask is:

'How can I tell this person who is a dear friend, colleague, or relative of mine, I believe they have a mental health problem – without them *taking* offence, *feeling* insulted, or *becoming* alienated from me?'

There are, of course, a number of ways to do this, but in this newsletter edition, we will focus on the first option. Further options will follow in subsequent editions.

Here are some important considerations not to be overlooked

1) Approach (as a caring friend *vs.* an accusing bystander)
2) Choice of language (affirming and conciliatory *vs.* provocative)
3) Setting (relaxed and quiet *vs.* distracting or disruptive)
4) Attitude (of genuine interest and support vs. 'you're on your own')
5) Suggestion ready (name and contact info. to a psychologist or psychiatrist, *both* a male and a female)

Approach. Be sure to clearly project your feelings of caring and concern. Let your face convey such expressions with a mild, softened seriousness, and your voice tone should be pleasant and non-threatening, *particularly*. Give that person your undivided attention should they ask for clarification, offer questions, or make comments, with ongoing eye contact (and natural turning away, periodically, so as not to create discomfort), and the reassuring touching of another's hand, where relationship-appropriate. This sets the stage for the best possible encounter and outcome. You'll not be seen as an 'outsider' pointing your finger at them, but more likely as a 'comrade' standing with them.

Choice of Language. Since many people object to labels for the negative connotations they can convey, and interpret them as provocative (inviting a defensive stance, if not a 'counterattack'), there is no need to use such words as, 'Obsessive Compulsive Personality Disorder', 'OCPD', 'mental illness', 'personality disorder', 'personal problem', or the like, *at all*, when sharing your concerns with the OCPD person. Even the words 'psychologist' and 'psychiatrist' need *not* be spoken. Speak **only** those words and phrases that convey a recognition of, and primary focus upon achieving and maintaining, **psychological health and wellness**, as opposed to psychological disturbance or mental illness. This, along with your affirming and conciliatory words (examples which follow in **blue highlight**) will all serve to create as pleasant an interaction as possible with the OCPD person.

Setting. The surroundings where you choose to talk with the OCPD person about their condition can be of paramount importance, as this person *will not likely forget* the place and time of your broaching this very sensitive topic. If the locale is one of relaxation and beauty, comfortableness and desirability, quiet and non-distracting, then these positive qualities will be, if only unconsciously, permanently associated in the OCPD person's mind with your bringing up of the topic and your mutual discussion. This, clearly, can have a favorable impact upon their receptivity to your concerns, and whether or not the OCPD person will adopt a viewpoint of 'Okay, I'll willing to give your words some consideration.'

Attitude. Try as best as you can *not* to exhibit an attitude, or *disposition*, of upset, discomfort, apprehension, or nervousness when you talk with the OCPD person, as they will definitely pick up on this, and reflect it back to you, automatically. Instead, strive to embody and project the qualities of genuine voluntary interest and desire to support them, to stand by them, versus involuntary forced attention to them due to their unwelcome annoying of you, other household members, or workplace associates. (And since fear often underlies any hesitation to approach them, just prior to your meeting with them, you might mentally recite the following affirmation: 'I am completely **safe** and **secure** and **calm** around [Mary, Tom, or Christine, etc.], *no matter <u>how</u> they respond to me.*')

<u>Suggestion Ready</u>. Do some research, beforehand, and locate both a *male* and *female* mental health practitioner who are qualified to recognize and treat OCPD. You will likely need to phone them to be certain of this, visiting them would even be better to better evaluate their suitability. (Remember, too, since 25 percent of OCD people also have OCPD, you may need to start your search with psychologists or psychiatrists who treat <u>OCD</u>, as they surely must deal with the 'co-morbid' condition of OCPD, of necessity, as well.) And, by having both genders to choose form as an option, your OCPD friend can choose the gender they feel most comfortable with eventually sharing intimate details of their life.

Further instructions on how best to tell the OCPD person of your concerns:

First, schedule your 'sharing' session with the OCPD person at a time of their convenience, where the two of you can sit down together, where you both will be comfortable, will not be disturbed, and where there will be no interruptions (turn off cell phones and/or mute the land-line). Perhaps the two of you could dine out together, in a comfortable and relaxed setting, and afterward, you could broach the subject of their disorder, but not necessarily mentioning the name of their disorder (or even that it *is* a disorder as mentioned above). Be sure that the OCPD person is in a fairly good mood at the time. Then, start out by thanking her or him for their having taken the time to meet with you, spend some time with you, *reassuring* this person of your care and concern for their well-being, and of your appreciation for them. This is the best place to start.

Take the following scenario, for example:

'Mary, thanks so much for meeting with me. I appreciate it, and I appreciate you. I wanted to tell you that because **I value you, and want the best for you, I want you to be as happy as you can be.**

'But, I am growing increasingly more concerned for **your** happiness and well-being. I've noticed that you often seem to be unhappy, or upset, or not in the best mood. Also, that you often seem preoccupied, impatient, worried, irritable, and even argumentative. Are you aware that you are often acting like this? (If they say, 'no', you can suggest that they check with others to see whether those others see this, as well.)

'Further, **and I know you mean well**, but you have a tendency to tell other people what to do, or how to do it, or when; and you often insist upon your own way. [Notice, you are affirming their right intention]

'I just want you to know that I think **you might consider** talking with a trusted friend about this, or better still, **talk with a <u>counselor</u>** who may be able to help **you** determine precisely what is bothering you so, or keeping you the way you are, and then **you** could decide upon ways to change this so **you** might become more happy and at peace. [no need to say the words 'psychologist' or 'psychiatrist' at this time]'

Once you have arrived at this point in your conversation, be prepared to encounter, even though you have been so conciliatory and appreciative, resistance, surprise, upset, even anger. Nonetheless, you have responsibly informed them out of love and concern, and have planted the 'seed' for their further thought.

This direct approach has the advantage of letting your loved one or friend know that you, *personally*, believe this matter needs attention, and that should this person be told by another that <u>you</u> suspected this, the OCPD person might accuse you of being secretive or even dishonest with them.

Next month, we'll discuss the <u>merits</u> of having *another* person broach the topic with the OCPD person.

Till next time,

Sincere Well Wishes,

Mack W. Ethridge
Founder and President,
New Frontier Health Research, Inc.
Shenandoah Valley, Virginia

P.S.: To the author's knowledge, only <u>one</u> other full-length book (301 pages) has been written on OCPD to date. This book is entitled **'Obsessive-Compulsive Personality Disorder, Understanding the Overly Rigid, Controlling Person'**, by Dr. Martin Kantor, MD., who is a Harvard-trained psychiatrist. You may learn more about this book by going to his book description at Amazon.com. There you will also find my posted review of his book. It has its merits, but is deficient in practical help.

DISCLAIMER: No recommendations within this newsletter are to be construed as medical advice, but only as educational reference material. Embarking upon any psychological or bodily health venture should be discussed with and overseen by one's personal mental health practitioner or physician. Author disavows all responsibility for use or misuse by newsletter recipient, or their loved ones, of research material herein.

NEW FRONTIER RESEARCH

OCPD MONTHLY NEWSLETTER

The **Golden Guiding** Principle

Escaping Another's OCPD Tyranny!

Solving the Puzzle

Gift Edition No. 2

Dear Friend and Fellow Journeyer,

A question loved ones, friends, and concerned associates of OCPD people often ask me is:

'If there is a Principle of Interaction that stands out <u>above</u> <u>all</u> <u>the</u> <u>rest</u> which should be observed when dealing with an OCPD person, which will afford the most <u>immediate</u> 'gain' to the non-OCPD person, in terms of maintaining one's peace of mind <u>and</u> domestic tranquility, *what is that Principle?*'

I am happy to tell you there IS such a Principle! And I call it 'The Golden Guiding Principle.' It is a very **fundamental** 'rule of engagement' that, *if* you are not careful, you may not give due consideration to, and thereby, forfeit the protective benefit it invariably imparts. So, let's begin:

Observance of THIS one principle of interaction (actually, the **primary** 'rule of engagement') with an OCPD person, *alone*, will save you untold moments and hours of grief and regret! (I know from first-hand, repeated experience with my OCPD loved one, and I am STILL becoming proficient in its use!) This is so because prior to speaking **anything** to an OCPD person, you should pause long enough to ask yourself whether or not what you have to say will serve as a trigger to their automatic, dysfunctional, negativistic replies, and then reflect upon the likelihood of that happening. Below is the concept in brief reminder form:

> The **Golden Guiding** Principle
> Before responding to an OCPD person, reflect 3 to 5 times *longer* than you normally would, on your statement or answer – **prior** to speaking it.
> (You'll be **glad** you did!)

Ask yourself *'Would the topic and choice of words I am about to speak naturally 'lead' the OCPD person down a particular path of response if she is prone to go that way?'* In other words, you need to think whether or not what you have proposed to say will serve as an 'open doorway' for the OCPD person to walk through, along with their darkened assessments and unbalanced, depreciating judgments. This time of pausing and reflection may extend anywhere from **30 seconds** to <u>several</u> **minutes**, depending upon the nature, importance, and possible 'volatility' of the topic you intend to introduce.

A helpful rule of thumb is that if after careful reflection you are still undecided, it is best <u>not</u> to voice it, at least not in the manner you first envisioned. You are likely to find, too, that *initially* it will be difficult for you to **remember** to pause before you speak to the OCPD person. This is natural, as when speaking to any other person who is psychologically healthy, you do not have to be so vigilant, so 'on guard'. But, here, it is quite a different matter! And the Good News is, with determined practice, remembering to pause will become a habit. So, strict adherence to this principle will help to safeguard your peace of mind from OCPD assaults as much as any other mental tool or technique. That is <u>why</u> it is called the 'Golden, ***Guiding*** Principle'! It will <u>guide</u> you to more 'peaceful valleys' of living. It is just that important! – And *just* that effective in helping to achieve your desired ends of avoiding conflict and subsequent misery. It will also sharpen your mental ability to detect (foresee) unwanted vocal interchanges and outcomes with anyone with whom you choose to interact, affording you the opportunity to prevent such a happening from occurring in the first place.

So remind yourself, periodically, throughout your day of contact or verbal interaction with an OCPD person: 'I will thoughtfully ponder the *advisability* of speaking about this topic, or voicing these particular words, at this time, to the OCPD person. And, if I suspect, after doing so, there is an appreciable (significant) risk of upset, disturbance, or conflict, resulting, I will refrain from that conversation.'

So often, in dealing with the OCPD person, it is the seemingly 'little things' that end up having the **greatest impact** on the quality of your relationship. Do not neglect to cultivate this habit of <u>thoughtful pondering</u> prior to any talk with him or her. It will pay you big dividends.

A second question loved ones, friends, and concerned associates of OCPD people frequently ask me is:

'What is the *best* antidote to my constant worrying over my loved one's OCPD condition, and the fears of our relationship steadily deteriorating, which so often intrude into my mind?'

Here is the optimal advice I can offer. The best antidote to the constant worrying you are so prone to do is to: (1) become **aware** you are in a mental worrying 'mode', and then (2) pause sufficiently long enough to remind yourself that *your worry is a traitor to your cause*, that of your overall well-being and welfare. A **key**, liberating thought is:

> Worry is a <u>useless</u> pastime, offering no real benefits

(Or, perhaps 'Worry is an <u>unproductive</u> pastime.') Due to old habit thought patterns, you will initially feel this is not true. 'Does not worry cause me to explore the problem,' you ask yourself, 'and search for a solution?' **No**, it really does <u>not</u>. Worry consumes your precious life energy masquerading as a benefactor, causing you to <u>repeatedly</u> imagine all of the bad things that are 'sure' to occur. Once you recognize this, you can **decide** to stop ruminating over your situation or challenge (as does a cow unceasingly chewing its 'cud', or regurgitated food), and instead make up your mind to take <u>physical</u> ACTION (<u>doing</u> something) to either alleviate or remedy the situation. Sitting around and just 'thinking' about the problem is a sure recipe for mental and emotional turmoil! Ponder your options, **yes**, consider your alternatives, **Yes**, evaluate what recourse is available to you, **YES**! But, do <u>not</u> dwell on the pros and cons too long. Set a <u>time limit</u> during which you can ponder the problem, then turn your attention to some other entirely different matter. If you wish, you can come back to your 'worry time' – later, and resume! This will help you break this bad habit, in time.

The following is a meditation I have found helpful in combating '**old man worry**', which I wrote to remind myself when I realized worry was occupying a preponderance of my thinking. Recite it once a day _for a week_, and then see whether or not it can 'break the hold' of worry – on you! (Thereafter, you will probably _desire_ to continue it, as needed.)

Worry is the Great Self-Betrayer

I now Know worry is my greatest enemy. It seeks to discourage and frighten me into believing **the lie** that preoccupation with a problem is mandatory. Confidence an answer exists, is the antidote. How deceptive is worry! It tries to convince me I should become apprehensive, uneasy, and afraid that so and so will happen, or that such and such will occur, or I will not be able to handle it. It never tells the Truth! **The fruitless exercise** of worry would have me dwell upon what _might_ happen, what _could_ happen, or 'worst case' scenarios. I maturely consider all possible outcomes, but I stay focused on solutions and answers. **I remind myself** always that worry is a clever adversary that stealthily sneaks into my mind if I am not careful. It tries to demoralize and terrify me with its unending recital of impending woe. I am not fooled. **I condition my mind**, _daily_, to recite and rehearse Truth statements, affirmations, and poetic verities, which strengthen my thinking processes to accept only a Vision of my Life that is Whole and Growing.

Worry is negative thinking at its worst. More so than any other thought or idea, it seeks to betray, and abolish, my natural confidence in myself, and my capabilities. **It is a liar _not_ to be believed. The false witness** of worry seeks to have me over-concerned with challenges, to have me become anxious and disquieted. But, I now Recognize its very denial of life, and refuse to buy into its hurtful tales. **I declare** mental and psychological war upon worry! I WILL not to fall prey to its falsehoods! As soon as any 'worry thought' intrudes upon my consciousness, I promptly reject it and hold to thoughts of calm.

By mental practice, I discipline my mind to reject worry as a foreign intruder to my natural, confident, positive mental attitude. With this attitude of being a winner, a problem-solver, I rise above worry, each day. **I refuse** to let worry dominate my life, and imprison me in its dark chambers. It is well within my power to remain free of its clutches, and live a life of self-assurance, confidence, and most of all, protecting faith in the Living God.

I trust this month's words of **Truth** and **Assurance** have strengthened and encouraged you as you confront the ongoing challenges of your loved one's OCPD. You ARE capable to meet them! – As you WILL see!

Next month, we'll touch on the merits and demerits of having *another* person broach the topic of OCPD to the Insight-lacking OCPD person.

Till next time,

Sincere Well Wishes,

Mack W. Ethridge

DISCLAIMER: No recommendations within this newsletter are to be construed as medical advice, but only as educational reference material. Embarking upon any psychological or bodily health venture should be discussed with and overseen by one's personal mental health practitioner or physician. Author disavows all responsibility for use or misuse by newsletter recipient, or their loved ones, of research material herein.

NEW FRONTIER RESEARCH

OCPD MONTHLY NEWSLETTER

Third-Party Approach to OCPD

Escaping Another's OCPD Tyranny!

Solving the Puzzle

Gift Edition No. 3

Dear Friend and Fellow Journeyer,

In a previous newsletter, we explored together the merits and demerits of _your_ broaching the topic of OCPD to your loved one you suspect has it, as a husband or wife, or even as a brother or sister, or the like. In this issue we will examine some important considerations of having a person _other than_ yourself, or even _other than_ an immediate family member, broach the topic of OCPD to one you suspect (or are certain) has OCPD. This following question, however, though introduced before, would also

...pertain to a mutual friend whom you had asked to speak to your OCPD loved one, so we will proceed from there:

'How can I tell this person who is a dear friend, colleague, or (*not-*immediate) relative of mine, I believe they have a mental health problem – without them *taking* offence, *feeling* insulted, or *becoming* alienated from me?'

Advantages of having a mutual friend broach the topic to this loved one having OCPD

There is a saying once voiced by a man of wondrous wisdom as follows: 'A prophet is *not* without honor, save in his own country and in his own house [or household, relative to his influence there].' By extension, this principle could be applied to say, perhaps, a husband and wife, where one of the two has OCPD, and the other (the 'prophet', or the one who bears an unwelcome message) would seek to inform that loved one of their mental health condition. Of course, most often, the mentally ill person would view their concerned loved one 'without honor' (with some exceptions). That is to say, without *respect* for what their spouse had to say, or, in other words, without *credibility*. For after all, as they see it, 'This is *just* my husband speaking,' or 'This is *just* my wife speaking.' 'No one especially qualified to make such an extraordinarily, even ridiculous, pronouncement – as if they were an authority on mental health issues!'

What is truly happening in such instances? Unfortunately, the dynamic of interpersonal **familiarity** comes into play, here, and such daily, close, life-interacting familiarity between two family members may well have lessened (or even eroded) the high regard one or both would normally have for the other, which should be maintained between two related people if harmony and goodwill are to prevail in that relationship.

Of course, beyond this is the bigger challenge, in fact, the biggest problem, which is lack of (or, poor) 'Insight', the technical, medical term being **anosognosia** – to be discussed at greater length in a future issue.

However, even given the above, there is a slightly greater chance that the OCPD person might be at least *partially* receptive to the broaching of this topic by a trusted and respected friend, or even a well-liked co-worker. (For remember, this friend of the OCPD person is *not* a person residing within the OCPD person's 'own house', leaving the possibility of 'honor', at least to some degree, being present between the two parties, as per the true observation of the man of wonder cited above.)

Whereupon, should that be the case, the OCPD person *may* be open to (1) reflecting upon the idea further, and discussing it later with their friend, or (2) being willing to speak to a counselor about the possibility of their having it, not necessarily a psychologist or psychiatrist, and/or (3) at least read literature (either articles or a book) that describes this condition and ponder its relevance to themselves.

Along with this, the concerned party, the friend or co-worker, would naturally adhere to the suggestions offered in the previous newsletter entitled **Telling Another They Have OCPD** regarding the Five Important Considerations of Interaction, as rehearsed in *abridged* form here:

<u>Approach</u>. Be sure to clearly project your feelings of caring and concern. Let your face convey such expressions with a mild, softened seriousness, and your voice tone should be pleasant and non-threatening, *particularly*.

. . .

Choice of Language. Since many people object to labels for the negative connotations they can convey, and interpret them as provocative (inviting a defensive stance, if not a 'counterattack'), there is no need to use such words as, 'Obsessive Compulsive Personality Disorder', 'OCPD', 'mental illness', 'personality disorder', 'personal problem', or the like, <u>*at all*</u>, when sharing your concerns with the OCPD person . . .

Setting. The surroundings where you choose to talk with the OCPD person about their condition can be of <u>paramount importance</u>, as this person *will not likely forget* the place and time of your broaching this very sensitive topic . . .

Attitude. Try as best as you can <u>*not*</u> to exhibit an attitude, or *disposition*, of upset, discomfort, apprehension, or nervousness when you talk with the OCPD person, as they will definitely pick up on this, and reflect it back to you, automatically . . .

Suggestion Ready. Do some research, beforehand, and locate both a *male* and *female* mental health practitioner who are qualified to recognize and treat OCPD. You will likely need to phone them to be certain of this, visiting them would even be more helpful to better evaluate their suitability (if, indeed, you are close enough to the OCPD person wherein they would not take this as intrusive or meddling) . . .

So, again, in summation, <u>The Five Important Considerations</u>

1) Approach (as a caring friend *vs.* an accusing bystander)
2) Choice of language (affirming and conciliatory *vs.* provocative)
3) Setting (relaxed and quiet *vs.* distracting or disruptive)
4) Attitude (of genuine interest and support vs. 'you're on your own')
5) Suggestion ready (name and contact info. to a psychologist or psychiatrist, <u>*both*</u> a male and a female)

Helpful and Encouraging Thoughts on the Nature of Insight

In Xavier Amador's landmark book, *I Am Not Sick, I Don't Need Help!* – 10th anniversary edition (available through Amazon.com), Dr. Amador lays out a program of how to help someone with mental illness accept treatment. I highly recommend this book as probably the best book I have ever read on the topics he covers. It is truly an extraordinary book, born out of his decades-long interaction with his beloved mentally ill brother, and his professional, life-long experience with mentally-ill patients as a clinical psychologist and a professor of psychiatry at Columbia University in New York City. And even though the book deals primarily with schizophrenia and bipolar disorder, I can't recommend it more highly as he addresses issues such as denial, uncooperation, effective interactive strategies, how to view and deal with the tremendous frustration and anger which can arise in yourself through contact with such psychologically impaired people, and how 'glimmers of insight' are real cause for hope, and much more. Further, Dr. Amador relates the most recent research (within the last few years) on the causes of poor insight, and what can be done about it. And, finally, he originated an incredibly effective approach and method to interacting with the mentally ill person known as L.E.A.P. (Listen-Empathize-Agree-Partner). It has been tested and proven with hundreds of patients, and many of its principles are transferrable to the OCPD context when used intelligently and with wisdom. Also, the concept of 'reflective listening' on the part of the non-mentally ill person is discussed in fascinating detail, and has proven to be a powerful tool for good. For more information, visit www.LEAPInstitute.org

Till next time, Sincere Well Wishes, Mack W. Ethridge

DISCLAIMER: No recommendations within this newsletter are to be construed as medical advice, but only as educational reference material. Embarking upon any psychological or bodily health venture should be discussed with and overseen by one's personal mental health practitioner or physician. Author disavows all responsibility for use or misuse by newsletter recipient, or their loved ones, of research material herein.

NEW FRONTIER RESEARCH

OCPD MONTHLY NEWSLETTER

How to Deal with an OCPD Person's – Personal Appearance Upset

Escaping Another's OCPD Tyranny!

Solving the Puzzle

Gift Edition No. 4

Dear Friend and Fellow Journeyer,

In this issue we will explore a common statement the OCPD person voices, believes, or offers as an explanation for certain behavior. To begin with, it needs to be understood that such people most often have <u>very low</u> self-esteem as they do not hold to the belief of **'Intrinsic Worth'**, or in other words, worth for *no other reason* than they are human beings deserving of respect, dignity, and consideration.

One such statement often voiced by OCPD women is: 'I don't care what <u>other</u> people think about how I look, but **I** care!' This assertion will often follow a discussion you may have with her after she asks you (with great distress, or uncalled-for seriousness, evident upon her face) 'Do you think my hair looks alright?' or 'How do my eyes look – are they too puffy?' or 'Does this outfit make me look frumpy?' etc. And no matter what your reply, this dear person will immediately discount any positive, supportive statement you make, and she will insist that she does look 'a fright'!

Then, of course, you may have assured her that most people are *far* too concerned about their <u>own</u> interests and concerns and life that they hardly ever pay much attention at all to another's hairstyle, facial appearance, or state of dress. They may note it in passing, but they give it no further thought, and they certainly do not judge or condemn another for it! <u>It is just not relevant to them</u>. It has no impact upon their life.

Also, you may have told her the majority of people routinely and automatically give allowance to others for *however* they look knowing that variation in grooming, the look of one's face, or choice of clothing are all occasioned by many factors. Nothing to be worried over, or concerned about, ever. But, this, too, seldom works.

So, what often happens when you say to the OCPD person there is really no need to be concerned with what other people think (due to the above true rationale), she (or he) may even angrily say 'No, as I said, I don't care what other people think about how I look, but I am concerned because **I** care about me!'

But, of course, that is not true. For if the OCPD person **really** cared about themselves, <u>that</u> would take precedence over their appearance, and such a person would not upset and distress themselves over so small a matter (comparatively speaking) as appearance – over the far greater value of and desirability of fostering one's mental well-being. After all, it is not the appearance (good or bad) that confers **worth** upon a person, but the mere fact of their personhood, as a unique, distinct, irreplaceable being made in the image of God.

It is the OCPD person's inability to make this crucial distinction that *self-condemns* them to fearful thinking that they will appear undesirable, lacking in taste, stupid, or ignorant.

Given the above, be aware of this faulty mindset whenever your OCPD loved one or friend exhibits these speech patterns reflecting this aspect of a faulty thinking style. Do not attempt to convince her otherwise. Do not attempt to show her the error of her thinking by telling her to do whatever she can, when she can, to 'fashion' her appearance as she may desire, and that there is no reason why she should trouble herself about this matter until such time and opportunity as she can make a change. She will not listen! Or, perhaps, better said, she *wills* not to hear!

The reality is she is simply locked into this misconception of herself, due to her OCPD condition, lacking the necessary **Insight** to see through or past this fallacy, which would free her from unnecessary distress, unease, and particularly painful self-consciousness.

And just remember, it is not your responsibility to convince her otherwise, and indeed, you cannot even if you try! This will spare YOU considerable distress by recognizing this. You may choose to disengage yourself from a conversation centering upon the OCPD person's appearance by simply saying,

> *'I like you [or love you] and value you any way you are.'*

And, then, leave it at that. (Although you may need to repeat this statement until such time as the OCPD person discontinues her tirade.)

It is this 'unconditional acceptance' by you of their appearance that may, just *may*, in the long run, help this dear person to accept themselves, their humanity, and the 'perfect imperfection' all that implies! For one cannot look one's best at all times, nor is there any need to! – A simple fact of life.

Of course, the OCPD person's feelings are arising, too, from their mistaken belief that everything needs to be 'Perfect' (as they define it) – especially their person! And, if not, they feel they become undeserving as they have committed an unpardonable sin! Bless them!

One Other Distressing Idea OCPD People Frequently Dwell Upon and 'Graciously' Share with You – Their *Terror* of the World!

OCPD people, especially more so with women, often have an entrenched 'fear mentality'. This fear begins with themselves (as with an *over*-concern with their appearance as discussed above) and extends to the whole world (as in all of the horrible and unfortunate things that are daily occurring to people in the world).

A number of these dear people will come right out and tell you 'I am *terrified* of the world!', or 'Our government leaders are doing nothing about safeguarding our rights as Americans', or 'Our nation is going to be attacked and we are going to be made slaves!', or 'I am afraid of an imminent financial collapse!' And, on and on it goes.

As in the first part of this issue, the same recommendation applies: It is best *not* to discuss these matters in depth with the OCPD person as their fear is unreasoning and reflexive. Even with reassurances to the contrary, the OCPD person will discount them and probably turn on you **accusing you** of not having a heart toward suffering people worldwide, or that you are being complacent about our national situation, or that there must be something terribly wrong with you not to get upset about all of this.

A helpful statement to recite to the OCPD person when this type of conversation is begun by them is:

**'I am concerned about the welfare of others,
but *my* becoming upset will <u>not</u> help the situation.
It will only <u>add</u> to the fear and suffering of the world.'**

Then, attempt to change the subject, or if need be, walk away from the OCPD person. For even attempting to persuade the OCPD person that so many of their concerns are unlikely to happen, or even if some of them did, they would be able to deal with it, will not quiet their fears at all. Again, it is in the nature of their disorder to anticipate and see the worst! You can further say, **'I will do whatever is in my power to prevent any of these situations from occurring, but beyond that, I refuse to worry or fear.'**

Till next time, Sincere Well Wishes,

Mack W. Ethridge

DISCLAIMER: No recommendations within this newsletter are to be construed as medical advice, but only as educational reference material. Embarking upon any psychological or bodily health venture should be discussed with and overseen by one's personal mental health practitioner or physician. Author disavows all responsibility for use or misuse by newsletter recipient, or their loved ones, of research material herein.

PS: Greg, I continue to pray for your family. Have faith, brother, but *tempered*, realistic faith. Things will work out for the personal growth of all – in the end. In God's Love, Mack

NEW FRONTIER RESEARCH

OCPD MONTHLY NEWSLETTER

The Hidden, yet *True Opponent* in Your Encounters with an OCPD Person

Escaping Another's OCPD Tyranny!

Solving the Puzzle

Gift Edition No. 5

Dear Friend and Seeker of Genuine Answers,

If you are keenly observant when dealing with a close friend, a loved one, a relative, or a spouse, who has OCPD to (*if* you are not careful!) an exasperating, if not infuriating degree, you will have noticed that this dear person actually seems to be *'possessed'* by a power, an energy, or a force, if you will, that has them <u>under its control</u>. This 'something' is **compelling** them to act contrary to their own best interests, to foment strife and contention, and to generate the GREATEST disharmony, ill-will, and even aggression toward another. In short, to **destroy** healthful, life-affirming, beneficial, human- and God-honoring relationships.

Take the time to notice their facial expressions, and their eyes, *particularly*, which fairly proclaim their total immersion in, and/or captivity to, this 'field' of harmful and disruptive **Intention**. Observe how this person is virtually reciting, in rote, without thinking, even as an automaton, words and concepts and viewpoints that are blatantly *illogical*, *nonsensical*, and *contrary to sound, healthful psychological principles and reality*! Notice how oblivious such an OCPD person is to this FACT, irrespective of whether you clearly, and *lovingly*, point this out to them.

Once you deliberately set out to do this mental observational exercise, and it only takes a few times, it is truly eye-opening; and most certainly is so, if you have never viewed it from this standpoint before. Also, don't be surprised if you are a bit *startled*, as **Truth**, Life-Transforming **TRUTH**, often has a way of commanding a person's attention so that the message is powerfully conveyed to their consciousness to foster permanent mental retention for the good of the receiver.

Now, I'll repeat this, once more, as it bears repeating: It will become apparent, with careful observation, that this dear soul is *not* acting rationally, *not* interacting sanely, and most assuredly is *NOT* exercising their **free-will volition**, which would allow them: 1) to pause and *question* their position, 2) *entertain* different views, and, 3) *analyze* the soundness of their position, or stance. *It is as though these capacities have been stripped from them*, leaving them helpless to propagate the **ill-intentions** and **ill-will** and **negative energies** of someone else, or *something* else; again, all unbeknownst to their normal surface awareness. It is as though a shroud, or a covering of some type, had been cast over their minds,

blinding them to the harm and destructiveness they are spreading. And *if* you, the non-OCPD person, have interacted only a *few* times with an OCPD person who exhibits **full-blown** characteristics and traits, then you **KNOW** the above description is no mere exaggeration!

So, *what*, in Heaven's Name, is actually transpiring here?

The answer to this question, and there *IS* a definitive Answer, is that one can only entertain it, and accept it, if you truly have an open mind, are an independent thinker, and possess a searching, fearless heart. Otherwise, **the Answer** will *forever* elude you (as you will reject it), and solutions you so earnestly seek will forever be beyond your grasp.

So, without any further delay, here it is:

It can be categorically stated, with absolute certainty, that the scenes you, as the non-OCPD person, are routinely witnessing, and enduring, the occurrences that are playing out right before your eyes, are *manifestations of the influence, direction, or even control of malevolent powers, intelligences, or entities*. This does NOT necessarily mean POSSESSION, in fact, in the **large majority** of the cases, it is *not*. Rather, the behaviors (even bordering on hostility) of OCPD persons are clear instances of **STRONG INFLUENCE** by what I call a Spirit of Anti-Life, Anti-Love, Anti-Good, and Anti-God!

The OCPD person, then becomes, an unknowing and unwilling (in the sane part of their mind) **actor** – performing those actions which alienate the OCPD person to virtually anyone they come into contact with, and create mental and emotional havoc within their respective circles, such as professional, recreational, familial, etc.

And, here, I hasten to add, such an understanding IN NO WAY should cause us to be fearful of such forces, as those forces can exercise absolutely NO Power over us, as long as we do not **nurture** or **nurse**,

foster or **encourage**, **express** and **amplify**, within ourselves, as non-OCPD persons, the lower traits of human nature, such as anger, resentment, jealousy, envy, condemnation, criticism, hostility, negativity, and the like.

For it is _only_ when we, any human being, makes it **an habitual practice** to engage in these non-constructive and other-person disrespectful feelings, that the Anti-Life forces (whatever you conceive them to be) can **add** their negative energies to our own, _amplifying_ them to greater, and ever greater degrees. Causing us (as OCPD persons are so prone to do) to spiral down deeper and deeper into an escalating vortex of depression, despair, dissatisfaction, and really, dangerous frames of mind in terms of one's mental stability, emotional health, relationship strengths, and overall life-adjustment, satisfaction, and fulfillment.

Which is all to say that the OCPD person, him- or her-self, is NOT your true antagonist, not your real opponent, but, rather, is the unfortunate and misguided pawn being used by that _something_ other than themselves. That _something_ which seeks their harm and demise.

For those who are _not_ of the historic Christian faith, they may well call such a force an energy not understood or unknown life-form coming from _the para-normal realm_. Not a supernatural realm, mind you, but a realm science is just recently beginning to study and lend credence to. These respected researchers are called parapsychologists.

To the Christian, however, their Hebrew and Greek scriptures make it abundantly clear, the propagation, and _amplification_, of the terribly distressing symptoms of OCPD people, are clearly in the province of invisible, fallen (relative to divine, or benevolent, qualities) beings, and their involvement in the OCPD person's life is, without a doubt, a genuine reality. Such entities seem to _feed_ upon all such departures from love, and therefore have a vested interest in magnifying the same.

Now, **the Great Benefit** in recognizing the *behind-the-scenes* reality of what is truly transpiring here, is that the non-OCPD person can separate (in their minds and hearts), the poor, suffering OCPD person – from their harmful speech and behaviors, allowing one to **LOVE** them, the person; to **PITY** them, the person; and to have **COMPASSION** for them, the person; knowing that in a very real sense they are NOT responsible for their 'personality disorder'. They have been insidiously taken over by something *beyond* themselves. This realization brings a measure of **PEACE** to the non-OCPD person's heart who is forced to, or by loving choice determines to, interact with the OCPD captive. Such **Peace** as is so desperately needed by the *non*-OCPD person whose life is intertwined with the OCPD person whose very sanity has been ruthlessly and cruelly denied them, and their innate, divine qualities, suppressed within them.

May you, my fellow journeyer, on the path to a freer, fuller, more enjoyable life, independent of *any* OCPD person's life situation, find solace in the above exposition, and an encouragement that will allow you to experience *more* love toward the unfortunate OCPD person (though it may need be at a distance), and *less* negative feelings toward them as disruptors of your life, and the lives of numerous others.

Till next time, With Sincere Well Wishes, Mack W. Ethridge

P.S.: Detailed, extensive, documented research on the above topic is available in the author's books entitled: *When OCPD Meets the Power of God!* And *OCPD Bondage and Spiritual Warfare!* Available at Amazon.com

PREVIEW: **OCPD Bondage and Spiritual Warfare** follows on next pages

DISCLAIMER: No recommendations within this newsletter are to be construed as medical advice, but only as educational reference material. Embarking upon any psychological or bodily health venture should be discussed with and overseen by one's personal mental health practitioner or physician. Author disavows all responsibility for use or misuse by newsletter recipient, or their loved ones, of research material herein.

The True, *Underlying*, Perpetuating Cause of OCPD and Its Insight *Prohibiting* Power

Our best scientists, researchers, and psychologists, alike, are all at a loss to explain what is often *the total absence of Insight* in OCPD stricken people. **How is it** that these people, often highly intelligent and observant in many other respects, are so 'blind' to their own self-sabotaging ways? ***Why*** can they not 'see' what they are doing to themselves, and their fellows? **How can it** possibly be that what is so obvious to virtually everyone else, *they are oblivious to?* It simply just does not make sense. This, at present, is a great mystery at which investigators and deep thinkers are obliged to just throw up their hands, and turn away from – in stunned disbelief and perplexity. They have no answer, as the whole situation appears completely inexplicable!

Something is clearly prohibiting OCPD people from realizing the Truth about their behavior. It is as if a concealing, partitioning wall of darkness stands between them and Reality. Or, put another way, it is as if the OCPD person is viewing everyday life, its Reality, with extremely faulty lenses, obscuring and distorting what is directly in front of their faces.

The following are all proposed causes, or contributing factors, of OCPD: Poor or inadequate socialization, brain dysfunction or abnormality, genetic predisposition, etc. And these can all be factors – to be sure.

Yet, we are dealing with something, a mechanism or **compelling influence**, if you will, that renders a person's thinking distorted, negative and pessimistic, incomplete or partial, detrimental to one's self at nearly all levels, and which mechanism is *incapable of detection* (by the unsuspecting person, at least). It is 'cloaked' under thoughts, feelings, and impressions, which are made to 'feel right' to the OCPD person, yet are **absolutely wrong** in the sense of their deleterious effect upon the OCPD person, and those who are made to suffer along with them. How is this to be explained? What is shutting off the OCPD person's sight so effectively, so thoroughly? How are thoughts which are not *wholly* sane, made to appear sane, and be accepted by the OCPD person as true? And how is it that when irrefutable evidence to the contrary is presented, even by respected and acknowledged authorities, to the OCPD person, that their entire approach to life is backward and self-defeating, they *still* cannot see the falsity of their unjustifiable mental positions and behavioral stance?

The explanation, introduced earlier in this report, may surprise you, be unbelievable to you, startle you, and at first frighten you, but it is an explanation which totally accounts for every distressing symptom the OCPD person exhibits (particularly when in *full* and unbridled manifestation), and which others have to reluctantly, and often with dread, contend with. And this explanation accounts accurately for the OCPD person's total inability to extricate themselves from their predicament.

So here is, now, the simple, yet, all-enlightening explanation:

> **The True, Underlying, Perpetuating Cause of OCPD And Its Symptom Magnification *Is***
>
> The **tremendous likelihood** that the OCPD person is being influenced by *invisible, malevolent intelligences,* which were well known to the intelligentsia, and lay persons, of the ancient world[1]; and whose existence and nefarious purposes are plainly set forth in Holy Scripture, as unclean *spirits*, evil *spirits*, or **demons**.

And that is the plain, experientially, historically, and scientifically verifiable Truth! Which *proof* is available to all **progressive** and **free-thinking** researchers of **courage** and **integrity** – and a *passion* for the Truth.

Such entities were widely recognized in the ancient world by their learned scholars, doctors, and even scientists. These entities constitute another 'life form' antagonistic, even hostile, to humans, whose sole reason for being is to subjugate, torment, and enslave people who 'open the door' to their entrance, and 'invite' these entities into their person and affairs. They are bent upon destroying people, and the OCPD person is the way he or she is, because such spirits have **invaded** their person, usually by *directing* their thoughts (through establishing their **mental focus**) and influencing their behaviors through faulty beliefs and defective philosophical postures. These intelligences *encourage* moods of self-pity, pessimism, and negativity by *magnifying* such feelings (through adding their **negative energies** to the OCPD person's own). These malevolent entities then 'feed' upon the drama. End excerpt from **OCPD Bondage and Spiritual Warfare**.

NEW FRONTIER RESEARCH

OCPD MONTHLY NEWSLETTER

The Peril that <u>*Must*</u> Be Recognized and <u>Decisively</u> Acted Upon

Escaping Another's OCPD Tyranny!

Solving the Puzzle

Gift Edition No. 6

Dear Friend and Fellow Journeyer,

There is an **acknowledgment** and **recommendation** that is *seldom* voiced by writers on the topic of OCPD to the <u>non</u>-OCPD person. (And, I dare say, <u>*should*</u> it be voiced, it is probably done weakly and without the proper emphasis.) In fact, I have yet to hear it, or read it, by any writer, author, researcher, psychologist, or psychiatrist on the OCPD question. Either they do not understand the **gravity** of the situation (very shortly to be described), or they **lack** the **courage** and **forthrightness** to articulate it with clarity, conviction, persuasion, and power. A **'political correctness'** of sorts, is adopted, which *shies away from* the slightest possibility of a fellow human being taking offense at their remarks. Yet, how inappropriate, nonsensical, immature, and **dangerous** this can be, and surely *IS*!

I am talking, here, about **what to do** when confronting an OCPD person who has FULL-BLOWN symptoms, with *zero* Insight, and who possesses the **majority** (upwards to a dozen or so) of the disordered, negative, harmful, **primary** OCPD traits to a prominent degree – Those traits which so thoroughly identify and characterize the OCPD person. These traits include: Controlling, criticizing, complaining, worrying, negative outlook, orderliness (extreme), perfectionistic (pathologic), rule bound, conscientious (to the absurd), discerning blindness (inability to differentiate), inflexible and rigid, judgmental (to the 'nth' degree), along with being aggressively demanding, highly argumentative, and blatantly disrespectful. Even to the point of angry, irrational, 'persecution'.

So, we are NOT talking here about the clinically-diagnosed OCPD person who possesses only *three* or *four* of these traits (the minimum amount for a determination), which is problematic and distressing enough. Rather, we are talking about the unfortunate soul who is **ENVELOPED** *by*, **IMMERSED** *in*, and wholly **IMPRISONED** *within* – the world of OCPD madness. There is simply no way to describe this situation 'delicately' or 'politely' if one is to convey the severity and seriousness of the matter, and to impress upon the non-OCPD person the 'fury' he or she is facing!

But from this author, you **will** have it, however! – What *SHOULD* be told to the non-OCPD person seeking accurate, truthful, adult, mature, sober (serious), true-to-*Harsh*-Reality, education, counseling and guidance for their mental/emotional/and physical **protection**:

In the author's totally unique, courageous, and _keeping faith_ with the non-OCPD reader, book, **The OCPD Disorder – Its True Seriousness and _Unrecognized_ Peril**, he begins with the following:

An Open, Concerned, and Respectful Letter

Dear Reader,

The title of this book is NOT a sensationalist attempt to arrest your attention. Nor is it a clever tactic utilized to draw you into aberrational (distorted and discriminatory) thinking. It is not a title designed to frighten or mislead you. It is a title prudently (wisely) and compassionately selected to sincerely INFORM you of a **very real**, yet often _unrecognized_, _undiscussed_, and/or _underplayed_, **DANGER**, every OCPD interactor must acknowledge and face, _if_ he or she is to safeguard their mental health, preserve their emotional stability, and even to retain their most priceless possession – their God-bestowed **sanity** – their sound and healthy mind.

The title is designed to cause you to _stop_, _ponder_, and **carefully consider** its relevance to your life as you face daily interaction with an OCPD person. This book title was carefully and thoughtfully chosen to convey with accuracy, directness and crystal clarity the **CENTRAL CONCERN**, and wholly _legitimate_ concern, every interactor should entertain pertaining to anyone's OCPD encounters and life interactions.

You may wonder why I, as a dedicated OCPD researcher, devoted counselor, and accomplished author, would take pains to **emphasize** my genuine concern and even **apprehension** for those individuals who by necessity, or by choice, regularly interact with an OCPD person _on a daily, long-term, even intimately-close basis_.

Firstly, of course, it is because I harbor a deep empathy for those people who psychologically suffer at the presence and from the behaviors of OCPD persons (as I have in years gone by), and I naturally desire to alleviate their suffering and curtail their mistreatment.

Secondly, it is because OCPD-possessed people, those with _fully-blown_, **intractable** (take note I said those with FULLY blown, _not partial_ symptoms), take **great offense** at, and remain in denial of, their toxic and destructive nature, and of their ability to transmit their **contagion** to the minds of others (extreme negativity, criticalness, accusatory nature, dissatisfaction, bitterness, etc.). . . . [Continued]

[Obtain the author's book, **The OCPD Disorder,** 81-pages, for **full** disclosure of _all_ dangers you may face, and what you _MUST_ do to survive!]

Till next time, Sincere Well Wishes, Mack W. Ethridge

DISCLAIMER: No recommendations within this newsletter are to be construed as medical advice, but only as educational reference material. Consult your mental health practitioner.

The OCPD Wife and Her *Often* Disastrous Impact upon *Both* the Marriage Relationship and Her Motherly Obligation

The OCPD wife is in a powerful position to impact her marriage relationship and motherly role for either good or ill. Yet, most often she brings about disaster through her confrontational and adversarial ways.

The **five great evils** to which the OCPD wife frequently resorts to in her misguided attempts to get her way are: *usurping the authority of her husband, dishonoring her Creator, subverting her natural marital role, rebelling against her God-ordained purpose,* and *placing her children at risk of psychological disturbance.*

The first evil, usurping the authority of her husband, creates dissension between herself and her spouse. Her disputing leads to disharmony and strife. Often becoming adversarial to her husband, the OCPD wife refuses to follow her spouse's lead and submit to his authority as head of the household. She arrogantly presumes she has the right to 'override' her husband's decisions. The consequences are that by refusing to yield to her husband in matters of vital family importance, she violates the cardinal principle of 'unless two are agreed, they *cannot* walk together'. She perpetuates clashes and disrespect for God-ordained authority, undermining the sanctity of her marriage, itself.

The second evil, dishonoring her Creator, ignores God's admonition for her to be a 'helpmeet' to her husband. She fails to acknowledge the 'chain of command' where Christ is the head of the man, and the man is the head of the wife. Consequently, all this comes about by her refashioning herself into an unsuitable companion to her husband. She becomes 'derelict of duty' and no longer accords honor to where honor is due.

The third evil, subverting marital roles, compels the OCPD wife to take on responsibilities and decision-making tasks, and obligations, she was never meant by God to adopt; as she is temperamentally not constituted to do so on a regular basis. What happens is that the OCPD wife assumes the role of final decision maker, director of household affairs, and goal setter of the marriage independently of her husband's stated wishes. At some point, she no longer seeks his counsel.

The fourth evil, rebelling against her God-ordained purpose, enables her to cease being a helpmeet and supporter of her husband. She forsakes her role as the 'glory' of her husband wherein she would eagerly assist, encourage, compliment, and comfort him. The OCPD wife refuses to comply with her husband's legitimate and wholesome requests. And in so doing, *she abdicates her role of guardian of the household peace.* In the worst case scenario, she becomes a 'renegade' wife, no longer offering her husband his rightful allegiance. She opposes and competes with him, and she becomes a dissenter to the cause of domestic tranquility. She has, in effect, 'betrayed' her vows to 'love, honor, and <u>obey</u>' (conform to) the <u>Lord's</u> design (or plan) for marriage.

And the <u>fifth</u> evil, placing her children at risk, comes about by the OCPD wife modeling the role of a 'dissenting lieutenant', or second-in-command, and she showcases rivalry and challenge to the head of the family, creating an unstable and insecure environment for the children, and at best, a very 'uneasy' relationship with her husband. The consequences are that the sanctuary and haven the home are intended to be are dishonored and desecrated. The atmosphere becomes one of strife and friction, as the children become increasingly fearful, and are at <u>*severe risk*</u> of developing mental and emotional disorders of their own.

VITALLY IMPORTANT NOTE!

Scripture makes it abundantly clear that the husband and his wife are 'heirs *together*' of the Grace of Life'. Both are unequivocally EQUAL in His sight relative to their ***importance, worth,*** and ***dignity***, as 'bearers' of the Image of God. It is just that, in God's Wisdom, He has assigned different <u>roles</u> to male and female to guarantee a harmonious union.

(See *<u>corresponding table</u>* on next page for a correlation of all the above)

The OCPD Wife and Her Often Disastrous Impact upon Both the Marriage Relationship and Her Motherly Obligation
(*as* Scripturally Prescribed)

Evil	Outworking	Consequence
1		
Usurps Authority *of* Husband	Creates dissension between herself and her spouse. Promotes disharmony and strife. Often becomes adversarial to her husband. *Refuses* to follow her spouse's lead and submit to his authority as head of the household. Arrogantly presumes that she has the right to 'override' her husband's decisions. Constantly questions.	Refusing to *yield* to her husband in matters of vital family import, the OCPD wife is violating the cardinal principal of 'unless two are in agreement, they *cannot* walk together'. She is perpetuating a situation that guarantees clashes and disrespect for God-ordained authority.
2		
Dishonors her Creator	Ignores God's admonition to be a 'helpmeet' to her husband. Fails to acknowledge 'chain of command' where Christ is the head of the man, and the man is the head of the wife.	The husband is left without a suitable companion to further the best interests of the family. The OCPD wife becomes 'derelict of duty' and no longer accords honor where honor is due.
Evil	Outworking	Consequence
3		

Subverts Marital Roles	Takes on weighty responsibilities and decision-making tasks, and obligations, she was never meant to adopt. She is not temperamentally constituted to do so on a regular basis (short term and emergencies being the exception).	The OCPD wife assumes the role of *final* decision maker, director, and goal setter of the marriage independently of her husband's stated wishes. She disregards his stated wishes, and no longer seeks his counsel.
4		
Rebels Against Her God-Ordained Purpose	Forfeits her role of 'helpmeet' and supporter of her husband. Forsakes her role as the 'glory' of her husband (eager to assist, encourage, compliment, comfort). Abdicates her role of guardian of the household peace. Refuses to comply with husband's legitimate and wholesome requests. The OCPD wife elects to 'go it alone'.	Becomes a 'renegade' wife, no longer offering her rightful allegiance to her husband. She becomes an 'opposer' and a dissenter to the cause of domestic tranquility and harmony. She competes with him at every opportunity. The OCPD wife has 'betrayed' her vows to 'love, honor, and _obey_' (conform to) the _Lord's_ design for marriage.
<u>Evil</u>	<u>Outworking</u>	<u>Consequence</u>
5 **Places Her Children at Risk**	Models the role of a dissenting 'lieutenant', or	The sanctuary and haven of the home is dishonored and

atmosphere	second-in-command, and showcases rivalry and challenge to the head of the family, creating an *insecure* environment for the children, and at best, an 'uneasy' relationship with her husband.	desecrated. The atmosphere is one of strife and friction. The children become increasingly fearful, and are at *severe risk* of developing mental and emotional disorders of their own.

[Give] Honour unto the Wife,

as unto the weaker vessel,

and as being Heirs together

of the Grace of Life

(I Peter 3:7)

The OCPD Husband and His *Often* Disastrous Impact upon *Both* the Marriage Relationship and His Fatherly Obligation

The OCPD husband, just like his wife, is in a powerful position to impact his marriage relationship and fatherly role for either good or ill. Yet, most often he creates disaster through his dominating and intimidating ways.

The **five great evils** to which the OCPD husband turns to in his misguided attempts to sadistically subjugate his family members are: *misusing his authority as husband, dishonoring his Creator, abusing his marital role, corrupting his God-ordained purpose,* and *placing his children at risk.*

The first evil, misusing his authority as husband, is where he dominates and/or intimidates his wife, even deriving pleasure while doing so. He neglects to honor her as 'the weaker vessel', and fails to take her into his confidence through consulting with her on matters of vital family importance. The OCPD husband refuses to listen to her viewpoint, and give her it due consideration. He treats her as a servant, if not a slave. He makes demands of her, and will not tolerate disobedience, even if the 'requests' are demeaning, nonsensical, illogical, harmful, or dangerous. Consequently, the OCPD husband becomes a tyrant and a dictator. The wife is relegated to the status of a 'hired hand' or 'domestic servant'. There is no adult equality recognized. And the wife is often treated as an inexperienced child or an incompetent nobody. The OCPD husband issues orders and backs them up with threats in the form of verbal and/or emotional abuse. He may resort to physical coercion to achieve his ends.

The second evil, dishonoring his Creator, occurs when the OCPD husband no longer treats his wife with humility, kindness, respect, and manly gentleness. He no longer values her, and therefore, takes her for granted. He, also, by his actions, flagrantly disobeys God by not heeding the injunction 'husbands, <u>love</u> your wives, <u>*AS Christ loved the church*</u>'. Consequently, the wife feels disrespected, dishonored, disregarded, and abused. The marital relationship is severely damaged. And by the OCPD husband withholding honor from his wife, he does the same to God.

The third evil, abusing his marital role, entails the OCPD husband *not* providing for his wife's needs, and *not* offering protection. He *discounts* her needs and *withholds* protection, exposing her to harm by not inter-posing himself between problems and challenges *he* is constitutionally better equipped to handle and resolve. The outcome is that the OCPD husband does not 'look out for' his wife's welfare:

whether mental, emotional, bodily, societal, or spiritual. He simply does not care and neglects to provide, protect, and direct through dereliction of duty.

The fourth evil, corrupting his God-ordained purpose, is where the OCPD husband forfeits his overall role of *chief benefactor* to the family, and abdicates his role of just and compassionate *leader* and stalwart *defender* of the family. The OCPD husband has, regrettably, 'lost his way', and has adopted and *amplified* in his person the dysfunctional 'ways of the world', which are so detrimental to family health and life. Consequently, he no longer is fulfilling his purpose as ordained by God, and he now elicits fear and dread, instead of admiration and respect, from his 'household' kingdom. He has *inverted* his purpose to one of how cruel and callous he can be to his cowering wife and children.

The fifth evil, placing his children at risk, arises when the OCPD father reacts to his children with abruptness, dismissiveness, sternness, and harshness. He views his children, often, with disdain and as a nuisance. Consequently, his 'should be' beloved offspring no longer experience their home as a sanctuary and haven.

VITALLY IMPORTANT NOTE!

Scripture *clearly* places the **bulk** of the responsibility for the family welfare on the husband. He actually is *instituted* as the **'king'** (leader), **priest** (prayer warrior), and **prophet** (foreteller of good) over his family.

(See *corresponding table* on next page for a correlation of all the above)

The OCPD Husband and His Often Disastrous Impact upon Both the Marriage Relationship and His Fatherly Obligation
(as Scripturally Prescribed)

Evil	Outworking	Consequence
1 **Misuses his Authority as Husband** *as a family*	**Dominates** and/or *family* **intimidates** his wife. Neglects to honor her as 'the weaker vessel'. Fails to take her into his confidence and to *consult* with her on matters of vital family importance. The OCPD husband refuses to listen to her viewpoint, and give her due consideration. He treats her as a servant, if not a slave. He makes *demands* of her, often unjustifiable and unreasonable, expecting unwavering obedience, even if his requests, and demands, are demeaning, nonsensical, illogical, harmful, or even dangerous. May even threaten bodily harm.	The husband has become a **tyrant** and a **dictator**. The wife has been relegated to the status of a 'hired hand' or a 'domestic servant'. There is no interaction on the basis of adult equality. The natural, wholesome, love-engendering, life-affirming husband/wife relationship is destroyed, and the wife is often treated as an inexperienced child or incompetent nobody. The OCPD husband **issues orders** and will back them up with threats in the form of verbal and/or emotional abuse. He may resort to physical coercion and domination to achieve his ends.
Evil **2**	Outworking	Consequence

Dishonors his Creator	The OCPD husband no longer treats his wife with humility, kindness, respect, and gentleness. He no longer values her. He takes her for granted. He, also, by his actions, flagrantly disobeys God by not obeying the injunction 'husbands, love your wives, <u>*as Christ loved the church*</u>'.	Due to the OCPD husband's actions, the wife feels disrespected, dishonored, disregarded, and abused. The husband/wife relationship is severely damaged. By *withholding* honor from his wife, the OCPD husband does the same to God.
3		
Abuses His Marital Role	Instead of providing for his wife's needs, and offering **protection**, the OCPD husband *discounts* her needs and *withholds* protection, exposing her to harm by not interposing himself between problems and challenges *he* is constitutionally better equipped to handle and resolve.	The OCPD husband does not 'look out for' his wife's welfare, whether financial, mental, emotional, bodily, societal, or spiritual. He simply does not care and neglects to provide, protect, and direct thru dereliction of duty. He may 'push' her in harm's way with authoritative posturing.
<u>Evil</u>	<u>Outworking</u>	<u>Consequence</u>
4 **Corrupts His God-Ordained Purpose**	Forfeits his overall role of *chief benefactor* to the	No longer is the OCPD husband fulfilling his purpose

	family. Abdicates his role of just and compassionate *leader* and stalwart *defender* in the family. The OCPD husband has 'lost his way' and has adopted and <u>*amplified*</u> within his person (due to his mental disorder) the dysfunctional 'ways of the world', which are detrimental to family health and life.	as designed by God. He now elicits fear and dread, instead of admiration and respect, from his 'little kingdom'. He has *inverted* his purpose to one of how cruel and callous he can be to his wife and children. He has removed himself from the protective mantle of his God.
5		
Places His Children at Risk	The OCPD father reacts to his children with abruptness, dismissiveness, sternness, and harshness. He views his children often with disdain and as a nuisance.	The children, or teen-agers, no longer exper-ience their home as a sanctuary and haven. Their OCPD father has turned it into a place of complaints, threats, interrogation. All is never well, anymore.

Declarations of God's **TRUTH** <u>*Over*</u> OCPD
Power Thoughts to <u>*Overcome*</u> OCPD
I am **convinced** it is entirely possible for me to overcome my OCPD tendencies in a relatively <u>*short*</u> period of time. And, I realize I have **compelling reasons** to do so. I recognize that I have what it takes to succeed. And I <u>**WILL**</u> succeed!
New Frontier Health Research   Copyright©2015

Declarations of God's **TRUTH** <u>*Over*</u> OCPD
Power Thoughts to <u>*Overcome*</u> OCPD
I will procure <u>*whatever*</u> product or service available to me **proven** to equip people to <u>vanquish</u> their OCPD foe. I will record my progress in a **journal**. I remind myself that seemingly 'small' Victories are *stepping stones* to **Big** success! I will <u>review</u> these cards daily.
New Frontier Health Research   Copyright©2015

Declarations of God's **TRUTH** <u>*Over*</u> OCPD
Power Thoughts to <u>*Overcome*</u> OCPD
I <u>*genuinely*</u> and <u>*strongly*</u> **desire** to be set free from OCPD shackles. I, here and now, **claim** vibrant mental health as my natural **birthright**! I declare I am a *Rightful Heir* to a sound mind. And I **Vow** to persist in monitoring my thoughts <u>*till*</u> I achieve my freedom.
New Frontier Health Research   Copyright©2015

Declarations of God's **TRUTH** <u>*Over*</u> OCPD
Power Thoughts to <u>*Overcome*</u> OCPD
The looked-forward-to, resultant **Joy** of living in a continual state of **mental health**, <u>*free* from OCPD tendencies</u>, serves to <u>greatly</u> **motivate** me to become *ever-the-more-*mindful of the **quality** of my thoughts. I can and <u>**WILL**</u> become far more happy by doing so.
New Frontier Health Research   Copyright©2015

Declarations of God's **TRUTH** <u>*Over*</u> OCPD
Power Thoughts to <u>*Overcome*</u> OCPD
I am making the **conscious decision**, right now, to become **free** from OCPD urges. I <u>*accept*</u> this view as my Destiny! I **resolutely declare** myself to be OCPD free <u>now</u>! And I **commit** myself to this ideal. I will be <u>*consistent*</u> in my application of **True Thought**.
New Frontier Health Research   Copyright©2015

Declarations of God's **TRUTH** <u>*Over*</u> OCPD
Power Thoughts to <u>*Overcome*</u> OCPD
I will tell myself the **TRUTH** that I am <u>*wholly deserving*</u> of becoming free from OCPD. And that this Goal, <u>*once achieved*</u>, will be a **blessing** and a noble aim. My Success is a <u>**foregone** conclusion</u> and is <u>*NOT*</u> open to debate! I need only <u>persevere</u> to win!
New Frontier Health Research   Copyright©2015

Declarations of God's **TRUTH** <u>*Over*</u> OCPD
Power Thoughts to <u>*Overcome*</u> OCPD
In the depths of my being, I **Invoke** the **Spirit** of **Victory**. I recognize the time has come for my **deliverance** from OCPD to take place. I acknowledge <u>*my duty to myself*</u> to achieve this worthy Goal of mental healthfulness, and I am **committed** to <u>*becoming free*</u>!
New Frontier Health Research   Copyright©2015

Declarations of God's **TRUTH** <u>*Over*</u> OCPD
Power Thoughts to <u>*Overcome*</u> OCPD
I now choose to be **bold** in declaring that I will <u>*no longer*</u> tolerate OCPD characteristics. In fact, I **decree** with **absolute conviction** and **perfect certainty** that Success <u>**WILL**</u> be mine! It simply is <u>*not*</u> possible that I can fail due to the **strength** of my unconquerable desire.
New Frontier Health Research   Copyright©2015

Declarations of God's **TRUTH** _Over_ OCPD
Power Thoughts to _Overcome_ OCPD

I was _born_ with the **Innate Power** to _eliminate_ my OCPD foe. I **dare** believe this is so, because it _IS_ so! Therefore, I will act in behalf of my **best interests**, Trusting my **God-given ability** to _master_ this foe! I know my commitment _will_ overcome **all** obstacles.

New Frontier Health Research   Copyright©2015

Declarations of God's **TRUTH** _Over_ OCPD
Power Thoughts to _Overcome_ OCPD

I am **persuaded** that the life I desire, _free from all_ OCPD hindrances and obsessions, not to mention, _compulsions_, is **attainable**. I will _no longer_ believe it cannot be done. It **CAN** be done, and I am DOING it! I **CAN** change, and I **AM** changing, _becoming free!_

New Frontier Health Research   Copyright©2015

Declarations of God's TRUTH _Over_ OCPD
Power Thoughts to _Overcome_ OCPD

I am **persuaded** that the life I desire, _free from all_ OCPD hindrances and obsessions, not to mention, _compulsions_, is **attainable**. I will _no longer_ believe it cannot be done. It **CAN** be done, and I am DOING it! I **CAN** change, and I **AM** changing, _becoming free!_

New Frontier Health Research
Copyright©2015

Declarations of God's Truth Over OCPD
Fostering Accurate Self-Image

I can feel _utterly_ safe and _wholly_ secure in knowing that others' talents and gifts are _not_ a threat to me. In fact, I can **rejoice** in their good fortune, and I do! I **renounce** the errant thought that I am _diminished_ in their presence, and instead feel **great pride** in them.
New Frontier Health Research   Copyright©2015

Declarations of God's Truth Over OCPD
Fostering Accurate Self-Image

My **self-perception** has everything to do with my level of _life satisfaction_. I can know that I am **as good** as the next person, irrespective of my accomplishments or lack thereof. I am **valuable** for no other reason than I'm human, with unique **strengths** and **gifts** to share.
New Frontier Health Research   Copyright©2015

Declarations of God's Truth Over OCPD
Fostering Accurate Self-Image

Perfection actually lies within me and all about me, _if_ I only have 'wits' enough to perceive it. **I AM a _perfectly_ imperfect person!** _Seeming_ imperfection harbors a vital purpose and serves to **highlight** the **perfection** of my God-Like power _to accept_.
New Frontier Health Research   Copyright©2015

Declarations of God's Truth Over OCPD
Fostering Accurate Self-Image

I need _never_ doubt my worthiness to live life with **confidence** and **self-assurance**, because I am the **equal** to anyone and _everyone_. Not in terms of talents, to be sure, but in terms of **human dignity** and **rights**. And because of this, I can treat **all** accordingly!
New Frontier Health Research   Copyright©2015

Declarations of God's Truth Over OCPD
Fostering Accurate Self-Image

If I perceive my _role_ in life as one who is _entrusted_ with criticizing, blaming, and generally demoralizing others, then I see myself **falsely**. My self-image is flawed, and is _not_ in accord with **Reality**. Instead, I shall view myself as a **helper** and **defender** of life.
New Frontier Health Research   Copyright©2015

Declarations of God's Truth Over OCPD
Fostering Accurate Self-Image

_If_ I believe myself to be **worthy** of life only _if_ I perform 'perfectly', then I am misguided, and _self_-deceived. Never will I attain unto a **healthy self-image**, nor will I be able to appreciate _just how wonderful_ I truly Am. I, therefore, **renounce** falsehoods of perfection.
New Frontier Health Research   Copyright©2015

Declarations of God's Truth Over OCPD
Fostering Accurate Self-Image

A strong, healthy self-image is one wherein I **relinquish** _past hurts_ and disappointments, and **forego** future anxieties and _self_-manufactured fears. My **Great** Mind is _unworthy of such 'trivial pursuits'_ and wholly capable of **discarding** and living _above_ them!
New Frontier Health Research   Copyright©2015

Declarations of God's Truth Over OCPD
Fostering Accurate Self-Image

It is utter foolishness to believe I have to make another feel _badly_ or _inadequate_ for me to feel **good** about myself and **all-sufficient**. Any inclination I detect in myself to do this, I _ruthlessly_ 'exorcise' from my psyche and **expel** it! _I'll have no part in it!_
New Frontier Health Research   Copyright©2015

Declarations of God's Truth Over OCPD

Fostering Accurate Self-Image

There is no need for me to *inflate* my self-image through **exaggerating** my qualities and **exalting** my capabilities above others. I can honestly and forthrightly and proudly **declare** who **I AM**, without any sense of shame or embarrassment or fear! And **I will**!

New Frontier Health Research

Copyright©2015

Declarations of God's **Truth** Over OCPD
Protecting my Mental Health
Today, I will experience the **many benefits** of **mental health** ideals and practices when interacting with my fellow-woman and -man. This means I will extend to them a **highly respectful** stance regarding *their* autonomy and obligation to exercise it.
New Frontier Health Research   Copyright©2015

Declarations of God's **Truth** Over OCPD
Protecting my Mental Health
To be **mentally healthy** is to be clear in my view of myself, and strong in my conviction of its *accuracy*. To know that my mind can be, and **IS**, a citadel of strength when **I take conscious possession** of its vast powers for good in **upholding** others' dignity with grace.
New Frontier Health Research   Copyright©2015

Declarations of God's **Truth** Over OCPD
Protecting my Mental Health
To be *continually* critical of others is a **direct attack** upon another's well-being and mental composure, whether my criticism is justified, or *not*. This is a crucial concept to understand, as **grasping** it will **free me** from the prison of its poison circulating thru my life!
New Frontier Health Research   Copyright©2015

Declarations of God's **Truth** Over OCPD
Protecting my Mental Health
By looking on the **bright side** of things, I am proclaiming to Life that I **trust** It, and *believe* It is wholly on my side as a **son** or **daughter** of Its heart. So though I don't *yet* see the **full picture** of any given situation, I can **rest assured** there is behind everything an **ultimate** good.
New Frontier Health Research   Copyright©2015

Declarations of God's **Truth** Over OCPD
Protecting my Mental Health
To be **mentally healthy** is surely the greatest blessing one can have in life. It is a **prize** worth my fighting for, and a nourishing *environment* to be pursued. Even physical health cannot be compared to it. *For **mental health** will afford me **Peace**,* or True Power!
New Frontier Health Research   Copyright©2015

Declarations of God's **Truth** Over OCPD
Protecting my Mental Health
The possession of **mental health** will safeguard my *emotional* world, keep me **balanced** in outlook, and **calm** in intention. I *no longer* need self-create and experience turmoil *by clinging to fallacious ideas of life* as being dreadful and not worth living.
New Frontier Health Research   Copyright©2015

Declarations of God's **Truth** Over OCPD
Protecting my Mental Health
I take time, today, to salute whatever guardian there may be of **mental health**. For some, there is a *patron saint* who oversees this domain. For others, the **Living God**. But, I hail such a one for promoting its expansion in my mind, and give thanks for its sponsorship.
New Frontier Health Research   Copyright©2015

Declarations of God's **Truth** Over OCPD
Protecting my Mental Health
An important aspect of *protective* **mental health** is the firm conviction that I possess *more than enough* power to confront any disappointment with equanimity and an **undisturbed state** of mind. This includes when others fall short of *my* expectations.
New Frontier Health Research   Copyright©2015

Declarations of God's Truth Over OCPD Protecting my Mental Health

I choose to adopt, today, sound, constructive, **mental health** viewpoints, outlooks, and practices so that I might *thoroughly* *enjoy* *my* *life*, and be **an enjoyment** to all others I meet. My 'giving up' complaining is **a big part** of the remedy, which I gladly do.

New Frontier Health Research Copyright©2015

Declarations of God's Truth Over OCPD Protecting my Mental Health

To live as though others are **fully capable** of *self-determination*, apart from *my* unwanted interference, is a **life-enhancing** creed which serves *me* well. Others will make mistakes, and fail. But, this is all a part of the learning process designed for our highest good.

New Frontier Health Research Copyright©2015

Declarations of God's Truth Over OCPD

Protecting my Mental Health

To live as though others are **fully capable** of *self-determination*, apart from *my* unwanted interference, is a **life-enhancing** creed which serves *me* well. Others will make mistakes, and fail. But, this is all a part of the learning process designed for our highest good.

New Frontier Health Research Copyright©2015

Declarations of God's **TRUTH** Over OCPD
Ensuring Health Through True Thought
I can become a dynamo of **physical vibrancy** to an _ever_-increasing degree as I _one_-_by_-_one_ let go of anger, attempts to control, criticism, complaining, judging, perfectionism, and useless worry. For with **physical stamina** and bodily **strength**, I can _optimally_ function.
New Frontier Health Research   Copyright©2015

Declarations of God's **TRUTH** Over OCPD
Ensuring Health Through True Thought
How **wonderful** it is to know that the many health issues I endure can be dealt with _successfully_, often, with **True Thought** alone! Thought IS the 'Master Builder' as scientific research repeatedly confirms. That means, I am in control to a **large extent** of my welfare.
New Frontier Health Research   Copyright©2015

Declarations of God's **TRUTH** Over OCPD
Ensuring Health Through True Thought
Subscribing to **accurate thinking** about my _proper_ role in life, and how I can **best** relate to others, _is what overcoming OCPD traits are all about._ Headaches, neck pain, back trouble, digestive upset, even skin and muscle problems often are resolved by **thinking true**.
New Frontier Health Research   Copyright©2015

Declarations of God's **TRUTH** Over OCPD
Ensuring Health Through True Thought
I have at long last learned the **advisability** to think on 'whatsoever is **true**, honest, **just**, pure, lovely, of **good report**, virtue, and **praise**'. For by doing so, I erect a powerful _energetic force field_ all about me that promotes vibrant, robust, youthful **health**.
New Frontier Health Research   Copyright©2015

Declarations of God's **TRUTH** Over OCPD
Ensuring Health Through True Thought
The Mind-Body Connection is now a proven Reality. With _every_ **positive thought** I am promoting a stronger, healthier body. This is a proven **scientific** FACT! The more _distorted_ OCPD thoughts I challenge and **discard**, the _more_ healthier – and energetic I become.
New Frontier Health Research   Copyright©2015

Declarations of God's **TRUTH** Over OCPD
Ensuring Health Through True Thought
The emotional upset and bodily nervousness I have been so prone to experience while **captive** to the outpicturing of OCPD traits, I can actually now **forestall** and even _eliminate_. My mind controls my body, and here is where control is **warranted** and desired.
New Frontier Health Research   Copyright©2015

Declarations of God's **TRUTH** Over OCPD
Ensuring Health Through True Thought
The mental and **physical fatigue** I routinely experienced while under the sway of OCPD traits, are now _receding_ into the past! **Unburdened** by the heavy load of _false responsibility_ in taking on the burdens of the world has **freed me** to help more _intelligently_.
New Frontier Health Research   Copyright©2015

Declarations of God's **TRUTH** Over OCPD
Ensuring Health Through True Thought
Modern medical science has confirmed that dwelling upon the **positive side** of life experiences **creates an environment** where physical health will _best_ flourish. University studies one after another have verified this **central fact**. I now **choose** to make use of it.
New Frontier Health Research   Copyright©2015

Declarations of God's **TRUTH** Over OCPD

Ensuring Health Through True Thought

My body is continually **outpicturing** the state of my mind. If I want an untroubled and **pain-free** body, I must *encourage* and *cultivate* an untroubled and **pain-free** mind. Therefore, I will make *every effort* today to do just that, and **reap the rewards** thereby.

New Frontier Health Research

Copyright©2015

Declarations of God's **TRUTH** Over OCPD
Holding to True Appreciation of Money
Money is merely a tool, a medium of exchange. But, how I view money, and use it, impacts my life for good or ill. I choose not to *hoard* it, or *be stingy* with it, as this practice stops the **natural flow** of it into my life. It is *not* a scarcity, unless I make it so.
New Frontier Health Research   Copyright©2015

Declarations of God's **TRUTH** Over OCPD
Holding to True Appreciation of Money
I will be *responsibly* **generous** with both my money and my time, for in Truth, they are both the same. Through the glad *giving* and *sharing* of monetary resources, I create an atmosphere of **plenty** and **abundance**. Such a 'field' of plenty permeates my mind, too.
New Frontier Health Research   Copyright©2015

Declarations of God's **TRUTH** Over OCPD
Holding to True Appreciation of Money
I can *extend* the benefits of money to others, while the same time, holding them **accountable** for responsible use. Should any given individual prove unworthy of my trust in them and generosity, I have learned **profitably** *they* are not the best avenue for investment.
New Frontier Health Research   Copyright©2015

Declarations of God's **TRUTH** Over OCPD
Holding to True Appreciation of Money
Giving of my **valuable time** to others, in the form of *assistance, teaching, instruction,* or *encouragement*, etc., is an **excellent investment** in the all-important realm of human relations. Such time is never wasted, even if the person receiving such help *fails* to use it.
New Frontier Health Research   Copyright©2015

Declarations of God's **TRUTH** Over OCPD
Holding to True Appreciation of Money
The Great Secret regarding money is that it is meant to be **invested** in worthy endeavors and, *most* importantly, in the **service** of other people. One's family, friends, acquaintances, even strangers, as a gesture of love and goodwill. Wise spending yields **much** return.
New Frontier Health Research   Copyright©2015

Declarations of God's **TRUTH** Over OCPD
Holding to True Appreciation of Money
Money is my **servant** when I recognize it is meant to be a *tool* in my hand, wielded with care and **proper discrimination**, but never with a 'withholding' attitude that there isn't enough to go around. Money may need to '**grow**' for a time, but *once* grown, will spread.
New Frontier Health Research   Copyright©2015

Declarations of God's **TRUTH** Over OCPD
Holding to True Appreciation of Money
I now see the **wisdom** of *not* fearing money relative to the idea it must be 'locked away', somewhere, else it will lose its 'potency' and will cease to provide **valuable service**. A **preoccupation** of *fearing monetary loss* only tends to **bring about** that loss. This I will not do.
New Frontier Health Research   Copyright©2015

Declarations of God's **TRUTH** Over OCPD
Holding to True Appreciation of Money
Every investment of *my* time and energy toward another's welfare is never lost. That person may neglect to *make use of* my offering, but I will have had the privilege of extending help, and thereby, *will be the better for it.* My human bank account **grows**.
New Frontier Health Research   Copyright©2015

Declarations of God's TRUTH Over OCPD

Holding to True Appreciation of Money

I will **give** of my time, my energy, my money, and my resources (intellectual and property wise) for the good of *others*, and myself. For only the glad, responsible 'Givers' are *re*-**Given to** in **amplified measure**, sometime, by the Universe which **values** such giving.

New Frontier Health Research

Copyright©2015

Declarations of God's **TRUTH** Over OCPD
Bettering Home Life Relations
I will **remember** when interacting with a relative or sibling, should we be living *under the same roof*, my familial relationship does not entitle me to 'ownership' of them, nor authority over them. Though once a 'little' brother or sister, they are **now** adults.
New Frontier Health Research   Copyright©2015

Declarations of God's **TRUTH** Over OCPD
Bettering Home Life Relations
Relating to my spouse in the home setting in a *supportive*, *beneficial*, and *creative* way is **critical** to our mutual satisfaction as life partners. Comprehending this, I am careful to offer criticisms only in a **constructive**, **non-threatening**, low-key fashion, *if* necessary.
New Frontier Health Research   Copyright©2015

Declarations of God's **TRUTH** Over OCPD
Bettering Home Life Relations
I chose my beloved one over countless others as a life-mate. I recognize that part of my responsibility to her (or him) is to foster an environment of freedom of thought, expression, and choice. Only in this way, where there are **no domineering ways**, can we thrive.
New Frontier Health Research   Copyright©2015

Declarations of God's **TRUTH** Over OCPD
Bettering Home Life Relations
If I and my spouse are to live together *peacefully*, and *happily*, we both must become cognizant of the absolute necessity of **remaining positive** in each others' company. Negative remarks and observations tend to foster **discontent** and **avoidance**.
New Frontier Health Research   Copyright©2015

Declarations of God's **TRUTH** Over OCPD
Bettering Home Life Relations
No more important place exists than the home to foster better human relations. Better in the traditional sense of the occupants experiencing *acceptance*, **validation** of their ideas, and respectful *allowance* for their idiosyncrasies. To this end **I will strive**.
New Frontier Health Research   Copyright©2015

Declarations of God's **TRUTH** Over OCPD
Bettering Home Life Relations
My husband or wife needs to **know** that I am always 'in their corner', and am *always* persuaded to **further their growth** as an independent, self-governing individual. The **best way** to do this, I now see, is to *give up judging them* and to 'let them be', instead.
New Frontier Health Research   Copyright©2015

Declarations of God's **TRUTH** Over OCPD
Bettering Home Life Relations
Sharing living space with another human being can present special challenges. But, the **key** here is to recognize and then to overlook the *small*, really inconsequential, things, and pay attention to the **truly** *big* things. Only in this way, can **harmony** prevail.
New Frontier Health Research   Copyright©2015

Declarations of God's **TRUTH** Over OCPD
Bettering Home Life Relations
If I want to enjoy a **continuingly good relationship** with my significant other, I must learn to monitor and control what I speak to them every day. I must *take the time* to **choose** my words *carefully*, and **always project** the most *desirable* tone.
New Frontier Health Research   Copyright©2015

Declarations of God's TRUTH Over OCPD
Bettering Home Life Relations

As the great poet, Kahlil Gibran, wrote, 'we cannot give to children **our** own thoughts, *they* *have* ***their*** *own* *thoughts*.' And it is a good thing they do, else civilization would not advance. Apart from issues of safety, and clear moral choices, I will *not* impose.

New Frontier Health Research

Copyright©2015

Declarations of God's **TRUTH** _Over_ OCPD
Valuing Relationships Above All
I set my intention, today, to account the _quality_ of my relationships as more important than winning arguments, offering unsolicited advice, or verbally 'correcting' supposed mistakes of others. I **resist** these compulsions by seeing 'through' their harm.
New Frontier Health Research   Copyright©2015

Declarations of God's **TRUTH** _Over_ OCPD
Valuing Relationships Above All
I recognize, at last, the advisability of allowing other people **their right** to make mistakes, the freedom to try things their _own_ way, the personal liberty to experiment as _they_ see fit. As I would **most certainly want** the same consideration extended me.
New Frontier Health Research   Copyright©2015

Declarations of God's **TRUTH** _Over_ OCPD
Valuing Relationships Above All
I now carefully, with pleasure, observe that by adhering to a philosophy of individual personal freedom by **all people** to choose _their_ own way, I am set free _not_ to be **bound** to the distressing role of dictator, superior officer, or task master. **I can be free!**
New Frontier Health Research   Copyright©2015

Declarations of God's **TRUTH** _Over_ OCPD
Valuing Relationships Above All
I now **wholeheartedly subscribe** to the empowering belief that the Doctrine of political, religious, and economic freedom, _for which so many people have fought and died_, extends to the realm of _interpersonal relationship_ freedom. And serves **just as well**.
New Frontier Health Research   Copyright©2015

Declarations of God's **TRUTH** _Over_ OCPD
Valuing Relationships Above All
I now know that harmonious, cooperative, **satisfying** relationships are highly desirable above any _lessor_ desires to control or 'manage' another, which can only damage friendships and/or work relations. Therefore, I wisely choose to relinquish _lessor_ desires.
New Frontier Health Research   Copyright©2015

Declarations of God's **TRUTH** _Over_ OCPD
Valuing Relationships Above All
I am _so_ fortunate to now **know** that I can be _relaxed_, and _feel_ at peace while observing another person perform a given task or function in a way **I** would not choose to. That is ALL right! **All** are **entitled** to the prerogative of personal choice, even as I.
New Frontier Health Research   Copyright©2015

Declarations of God's **TRUTH** _Over_ OCPD
Valuing Relationships Above All
I now _genuinely_ believe the **liberating Truth** that honoring another's **personal preference** is **at the same time** honoring my own. No matter that I find _their_ preference dissimilar to my own. They are _not_ me, _nor_ am I them. _Their_ preference may precisely fit **their** need.
New Frontier Health Research   Copyright©2015

Declarations of God's **TRUTH** _Over_ OCPD
Valuing Relationships Above All
I wisely choose to be ever **vigilant** and **mindful** of any tendency of mine to _usurp_ the God-given rights of my fellow-woman and -man to govern their _own_ lives independent of my preference, otherwise. I do _not_ wish to find myself _in opposition to_ God's Will.
New Frontier Health Research   Copyright©2015

Declarations of God's TRUTH *Over* OCPD

Valuing Relationships Above All

I now fully comprehend I *cannot* expect **fulfilling** relationships with others *if* I **demand** of others to **conform** to *my* way of thinking, doing, acting, or being. All are individuals. *Each* (thankfully) sees things differently. To expect otherwise is foolhardy and naïve.

New Frontier Health Research

Copyright©2015

Declarations of God's **TRUTH** _Over_ OCPD
Enhancing Work Interactions
Working alongside of others successfully requires sophisticated interpersonal skills. Yet, the **foundation** is surprisingly simple – Respecting others' viewpoints _whether you agree with them or not_. That's the bottom line. Forgetting to observe this brings clashes.
New Frontier Health Research   Copyright©2015

Declarations of God's **TRUTH** _Over_ OCPD
Enhancing Work Interactions
Working alongside of others requires special sensitivity and maturity _if_ one is to do so enjoyably and productively. There is **no place** in the co-worker relationship for arrogance, superiority, or condescension. This includes demanding and insisting attitudes.
New Frontier Health Research   Copyright©2015

Declarations of God's **TRUTH** _Over_ OCPD
Enhancing Work Interactions
Today, I will make _every_ effort to work co-operatively with my fellow-man and -woman. Yet, I know to do this in a fruitful manner, I must not be a 'complaining Joe' or a 'woeful Mary'. Cooperation is encouraged by my **approving** statements toward others.
New Frontier Health Research   Copyright©2015

Declarations of God's **TRUTH** _Over_ OCPD
Enhancing Work Interactions
I _gladly_ allow others the freedom to make their _own_ mistakes so they may **learn** by experience. As long as I do _not_ perceive any threat or danger to their physical or financial well-being in their doing so, I will **not** _interfere_ with their God-bestowed right.
New Frontier Health Research   Copyright©2015

Declarations of God's **TRUTH** _Over_ OCPD
Enhancing Work Interactions
As a team-player in a place of business, I acknowledge my role to be one of _supportiveness, encouragement, valuing others_, and _promoting_ their professional well-being. This means resorting to praise over criticism wherever possible, and **gentleness** otherwise.
New Frontier Health Research   Copyright©2015

Declarations of God's **TRUTH** _Over_ OCPD
Enhancing Work Interactions
The Work Place provides the **ideal opportunity** to practice one's interpersonal relationship skills. Such skills as patience, attentive listening, allowing others to express themselves _without reprisal or fear of spiteful criticism_ is **crucial** for success. This I **choose**.
New Frontier Health Research   Copyright©2015

Declarations of God's **TRUTH** _Over_ OCPD
Enhancing Work Interactions
My place of occupation offers me the opportunity to grow in satisfaction, fulfillment, and **inner freedom** by _treating others as I would have them treat me_. This is _not_ empty platitude, but **powerful psychological and spiritual law**. I choose so.
New Frontier Health Research   Copyright©2015

Declarations of God's **TRUTH** _Over_ OCPD
Enhancing Work Interactions
As a supervisor of one or more employees, I take special care _not_ to **'trodden down'** the rights of those under my charge. I allow _as much freedom of personal expression_ to my people as possible, affirming _their_ highly individualized tastes and preferences.
New Frontier Health Research   Copyright©2015

Declarations of God's **TRUTH** _Over_ OCPD

Enhancing Work Interactions

Should my supervisor or manager **correct** my work output, either qualitatively or quantitatively, I listen with interest and attentiveness. I _no_ longer feel threatened by their observation and I evaluate it objectively. If they are right, **I can grow**.

New Frontier Health Research Copyright©2015

Declarations of God's **TRUTH** _Over_ OCPD
My _Invincible_ **Strength Against** OCPD
Within the storehouse of life-protecting capabilities in my mind, one stands out above all the rest. **Gratitude** is its name! Little did I realize that in the Presence of this **divine attribute** – all of those _tormenting aspects_ of the OCPD mind _begin_ to **fall Away**.
New Frontier Health Research   Copyright©2015

Declarations of God's **TRUTH** _Over_ OCPD
My _Invincible_ **Strength Against** OCPD
All of the uncomfortable, distasteful feelings of OCPD can be _negated_ by adopting the mindset of **Gratitude**. This is because **Gratitude** is the conscious focusing of the mind upon the _positive_ aspects of any situation, and being **thankful** for them.
New Frontier Health Research   Copyright©2015

Declarations of God's **TRUTH** _Over_ OCPD
My _Invincible_ **Strength Against** OCPD
To struggle unnecessarily against Life is to be _non-Accepting_ of its present appearance. I can retain my strong **Preference** that it _not_ be as it is, but I _choose_ _not_ to enrage or infuriate _myself_ by making OCPD demands (insistences) upon others unlikely to be met.
New Frontier Health Research   Copyright©2015

Declarations of God's **TRUTH** _Over_ OCPD
My _Invincible_ **Strength Against** OCPD
Along with Gratitude (positive focus) and Acceptance (decision to _preserve_ one's peace), the adoption of **Trust** that 'All will be Well' or 'Good will come out of this' will overrule the _false philosophy_ of the OCPD mindset that believes distrust brings happiness.
New Frontier Health Research   Copyright©2015

Declarations of God's **TRUTH** _Over_ OCPD
My _Invincible_ **Strength Against** OCPD
_No_ more psychologically powerful frame of mind exists than **Gratitude**. With it, I can _neutralize_ dissatisfaction, _dissolve_ discontent or unhappiness, and _banish_ OCPD thoughts that would darken my world and diminish my person. Being **grateful** IS _being_ joyful.
New Frontier Health Research   Copyright©2015

Declarations of God's **TRUTH** _Over_ OCPD
My _Invincible_ **Strength Against** OCPD
Another powerful mental tool that has the capability of _prohibiting_ undesirable OCPD expressions is **Acceptance**. To intelligently **accept** is simply to say, 'I will not _resist_ (strain _against_) this situation, but will peacefully 'allow it to be' – _till_ it changes, or I leave.
New Frontier Health Research   Copyright©2015

Declarations of God's **TRUTH** _Over_ OCPD
My _Invincible_ **Strength Against** OCPD
When I consciously **Accept** the 'Now' with its varied traits and characteristics, _though those traits be far from ideal_, I wisely _choose_ to retain my composure and dignity, and **conserve** my energy, which would be _drained_ with active, mental, OCPD _non_-acceptance.
New Frontier Health Research   Copyright©2015

Declarations of God's **TRUTH** _Over_ OCPD
My _Invincible_ **Strength Against** OCPD
I, here and now, forsake the _weakening_ idea that Life is against me, or is unwilling to support me. Instead, I hold fast to the _strengthening_ idea that Life responds, without fail, to _every ounce_ of **Trust** I give It. I then remain **Confident** (another word for **Trust**), and am rewarded.
New Frontier Health Research   Copyright©2015

Declarations of God's TRUTH *Over* OCPD

My *Invincible* Strength Against OCPD

My greatest strength against OCPD is the gift and strength of **Insight**. *Enough* **Insight** will eliminate OCPD tendencies effortlessly as the **Light of Truth** will illuminate the shadows of falsehoods, and the correct choice between the two can then be made.

New Frontier Health Research

Copyright©2015

Declarations
of God's **TRUTH** <u>*Over*</u> OCPD

The Central G O L D E N Key

I CAN and <u>*WILL*</u> become FREE of obsessive-compulsive tendencies and urges as I continually seek to acquire and expand my INSIGHT (Awareness, Perception, Comprehension) into the Great Laws of Life – *designed* for my greatest happiness and highest good. <u>*For this*</u> **I AM Grateful!** Amen!

Farewell Message

Dear OCPD Truth- and Relief-Seeking Friend,

This book has now come to a close. You now know somewhat of the author's **dedication** to teaching others *how* to meet the assaults and abuses OCPD would impose on you, and how to, with determined resolve and effort, strip OCPD of its power to harm, and cause it to cease to be!

It is my heartfelt prayer that you have found something of value in this book relative to **bettering** your relationship with your loved one who either has OCPD, or is the party in your union who is the non-OCPD person. Either way, both of you suffer, and it is not right that you do! Nor is it necessary that you continue to!

Therefore, for your relationship to be **reborn**, **grow**, and **flourish** as it was meant to, you will need every tool and armament at your disposal to confront your OCPD challenge, and to permanently **defeat it!**

But, this can **ONLY** be done with accurate, detailed, specialized, scientific, yet *understandable*, knowledge, the very kind of knowledge (and practical advice formulated from it) the author has painstakingly sought out, researched, and compiled in layman's language that *no one,* as long as they have a high school education, might find his material difficult to read or not understandable.

Or, worse yet, poorly presented, impractical, or ineffectual.

Now, then, is the time to **reread** this volume. Pause to reflect upon each passage, each instruction, each admonition. **Begin to put into practice** its recommendations, and *faithfully adhere to its outlined manner of engagement* with your OCPD loved one, or your non-OCPD loved one.

The future of you **as a couple** is at stake! And if this book makes sense to you, then by all means acquire other of the author's books, and LIVE the program! It **will** work, *IF,* you **commit** to work it! May it be so for both!

With Every Good Mental Health Wish, The Author

The **Relationship Restoring** OCPD Fundamentals

- Finis -

A New Frontier Health Research, Inc., Publication, Copyright © 2019

Special NOTE!

Be sure to obtain the author's book entitled, '**The OCPD Basics Study GUIDE, Relationship Restoring** – The **Companion** book!

Made in the USA
Las Vegas, NV
21 July 2021